Two in a Top Hat

Two in a Top Hat -

A Circumnavigation in Caprice

by Jan & Ian Mitchell

The Lakehouse Publications Australia

First published in *Australian Sailing* 1978, *Australian Sea Spray* 1978 and *Women's Day*, Aug. 1978.
Re-published 2012 and 2019 by The Lakehouse Publications, Lake Macquarie, Australia.

Copyright © Jan Mitchell and Ian Mitchell 2012.
Cover © Helen Marshall.

All rights reserved. No part of this publication may be reproduced, stored in a retrieval system, or transmitted in any form or by any means, electronic, mechanical, photocopying, recording or otherwise, without the prior written permission of the authors.

 A catalogue record for this book is available from the National Library of Australia

ISBN: 9780648497615

Printed on demand in Book Antiqua font point 10
by Ingram Spark, Melbourne, Australia.

Author's website: writingsfromjanmitchell.com
Author's Contact: jan.mitchell2021@gmail.com

Titles by Jan Mitchell available for purchase from the author, major book distribution channels and online distributors including amazon.com

Frontispiece

Caprice *on a cradle in Pittwater, soon after purchase*

Dedication

For our Grandchildren
Tasman, Tane and Kira Mitchell

Also by Jan Mitchell

tinker, tailor, soldier, sailor…the life of Colin Kerby, OAM

Crossings in Realitas: Part two of a Cruising Memoir
Hear the Ocean Sing: Part Two of a Cruising Memoir

About the Authors

Jan and Ian Mitchell 1974

Jan and Ian Mitchell bought *Caprice* in June 1973 and departed from Sydney at the beginning of February 1974 to sail around the world. When they reached Durban, they decided to have a child before setting out again. Baby Jamie was three months old when they sailed out of Cape Town harbour to sail up the Atlantic in February 1976.

After visiting twenty four different nations, *Caprice* sailed back into Port Jackson, Sydney on November 22nd 1977. Jan was six months pregnant with their second child – another boy they named David. Jamie had celebrated his second birthday in New Zealand, only two weeks earlier.

During the following year, Jan wrote twelve consecutive articles for *Australian Seaspray* magazine, another for *Australian Sailing* and the cover story for *Women's Day*. Ian also contributed an article to *Australian Sailing*. Those articles are reproduced in this book.

Acknowledgements

All the articles were published during 1978, for which Jan and Ian Mitchell retain copyright. Several of the photographs were taken by a photographer from Fairfax publications and have been reproduced here by permission.

The *Australian Sea Spray* articles were published in return for the free mooring of Caprice during the first year after our return from overseas. This was organised by Peter Dabbs, Editor of *Australian Sea Spray* and Mike Garrett, chief salesman for *Formit Fibreglass*, the company which created the moulds and manufactured the Top Hat yachts. Thank you to both of you.

Thank you to Merve Howlett, Lloyd Markham and Bob Cowdrey for information on the early days of Top Hat building.

I am indebted to Helen Marshall, for a beautiful cover design, to Tim Lamble for the map of Caprice's route around the world and to Dirk Visman and John Tylor for assistance with proof reading.

I would like to thank my husband, Ian, for minding our two young children in 1978, giving me time to write for the initial publications. I also thank him for technical assistance with organising photographs and inserting charts for this text.

Jan Mitchell 2012

This book has been re-formatted and reprinted in Australia. The content remains the same except for minor corrections.

Jan Mitchell 2019

Contents

List of Illustrations and Diagrams	ii
Interior Layout and Dimensions	iv
Map of Route around the World	v

Part One:

12 Australian Sea Spray Articles – Jan Mitchell	1
1 The Shakedown Cruise	3
2 The Voyage becomes a Nightmare	11
3 My Big Decision	20
4 Casting Off	25
5 Departing Australian Shores: The Indian Ocean	35
6 Meeting other Cruising Folk	45
7 The South Atlantic	55
8 The West Indies: The Windward Antilles	67
9 The Leeward Antilles	75
10 Off to the USA	83
11 Christmas in the Bahamas and Panama	97
12 The Pacific: Homeward Bound.	107
13 Passage Times	119

Part Two:

Women's Day Cover Story – Jan Mitchell	125
The Baby who Sailed 20,000 Miles	125

Part Three: Two Articles from Australian Sailing	141
1 A Cruising Awakening, – Jan Mitchell	142
2 Lost – Ian Mitchell	150

Part Four:

The History of Top Hat Yachts by Jan Mitchell	162
Addendum:	175

Illustrations and Diagrams

1	Top Hat Interior layout and dimensions	iii
2	Map of *Caprice's* sailing route	iv
3	Ian releases the mooring on *Caprice*	6
4	Jan and Ian hand steering	9
5	We were at the mercy of the currents	14
6	Loading up for departure	24
7	The QME wind vane steers the boat	29
8	Jan and Ian in the cockpit before departing WA	35
9	A red-tailed tropic bird	36
10	The RCA Dolphin engine electrics	37
11	Ian taking a sextant sight at sea	40
12	A lateen-rigged dugout leaves Port Maturin	41
13	Port Maturin, Rodrigues	42
14	Rodrigues' officials farewell *Caprice*	43
15	*Caprice* moored alongside *Naomi*, Port Louis	46
16	Korean fishing boats moored in Port Louis	47
17	*Caprice* moored outside larger yachts in Durban	52
18	We were guests aboard this tug boat in Cape Town	53
19	Jan and Ian on deck in Durban	53
20	Jan holds a flying fish	59
21	We sail under a spinnaker set with twin poles	59
22	James Town, St Helena	61
23	Jamie meets a Galapagos tortoise in St Helena	61
24	We caught a dorado (or dolphin fish)	64
25	Bridgetown harbour, Barbados	65
26	Trading schooners in Tyrell Bay, Carriacou	69
27	West Indies working schooner, *Baby Light*	70
28	Local boat careened on the beach	72
29	HMS Diamond Rock	75
30	Nelson's Dockyard, English Harbour, Antigua	77
31	Jamie explores unfamiliar stuff in Antigua– grass	77
32	The anchorage at Gustavia, St. Barts	79
33	Jamie's basket which had been his cot since Durban	87

34	Caprice on slipway, USA. Shows wind steering gear	89
35	Annapolis harbour during the boat show	90
36	Motoring in the Intra Coastal Waterway, USA	93
37	Navigational bridge, Intra Coastal Waterway	94
38	A large 'tow' in the Intra Coastal Waterway	95
39	Jamie in Florida (winter)	96
40	Speed boats creating heavy wash outside Miami	99
41	Route through the Bahamas	100
42	Looking back into Gatun Lock	103
43	Motoring through the Gaillard Cut	103
44	The gates open for us to leave Pedro Miguel Lock	104
45	A ship enters Mira Flores Lock behind us	104
46	A Galapagos turtle anti-fouls its shell from our hull	108
47	Anchorage within the lagoon, Ahé	111
48	A fishing hut on the reef at Ahé	111
49	Mama Fana taught us to make hats and baskets	112
50	Jamie on the beach at Moorea	113
51	The netball team at Taaha wanted to adopt Jamie	114
52	Anchor lines form a cobweb in Rarotonga	115
53	Jamie and Ian on *Caprice* at the CYCA, Sydney	117
54	Jan and Ian standing on the deck	123
55	Laundry, including baby clothes, adorns the cockpit	125
56	Jamie in his basket with his Mary Lou, a NZ toy	126
57	Ian and Jamie on deck, nappies fluttering above	128
58	The *Helenic Ideal* approached much too close.	129
59	Jamie sitting in the cockpit	133
60	Jamie in his backpack in the cabin	135
61	Jamie's new cot. The netting hooks to the deckhead	134
62	Jamie on his second birthday in New Zealand	136
63.	Jan holding baby David, Jamie seated alongside.	137
64	Caprice sails downwind at sea	141
65	Carbon blocked the exhaust pipe	148
66	Yachts moored in Whangarei town basin NZ	146
67	The photo *Australian Sailing* published	154

68	Ian winching up the mainsail	159
69	Jan and Ian Mitchell, 2012	173

Interior Layout

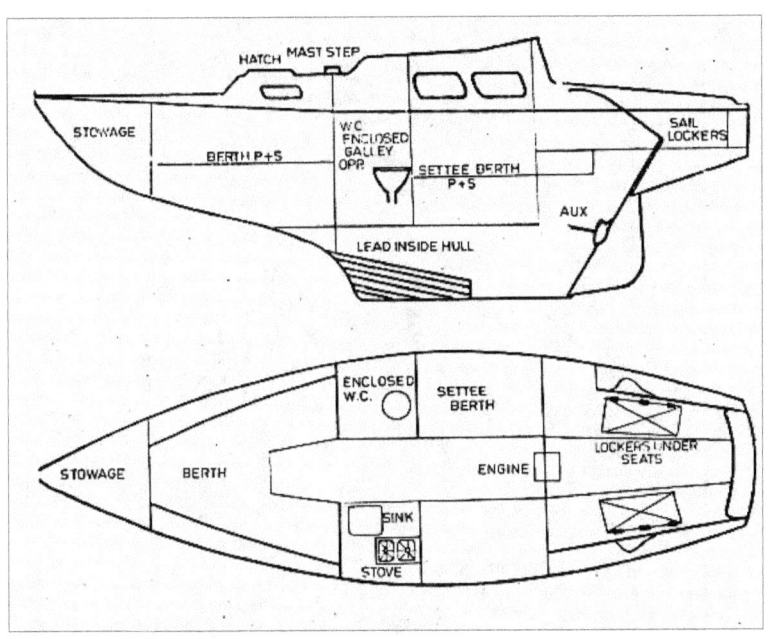

Dimensions

L.O.A., 25' 0" 7.62 m.
L.W.L., 20' 6" 6.25 m.
Beam, 8' 0" 2.44 m.

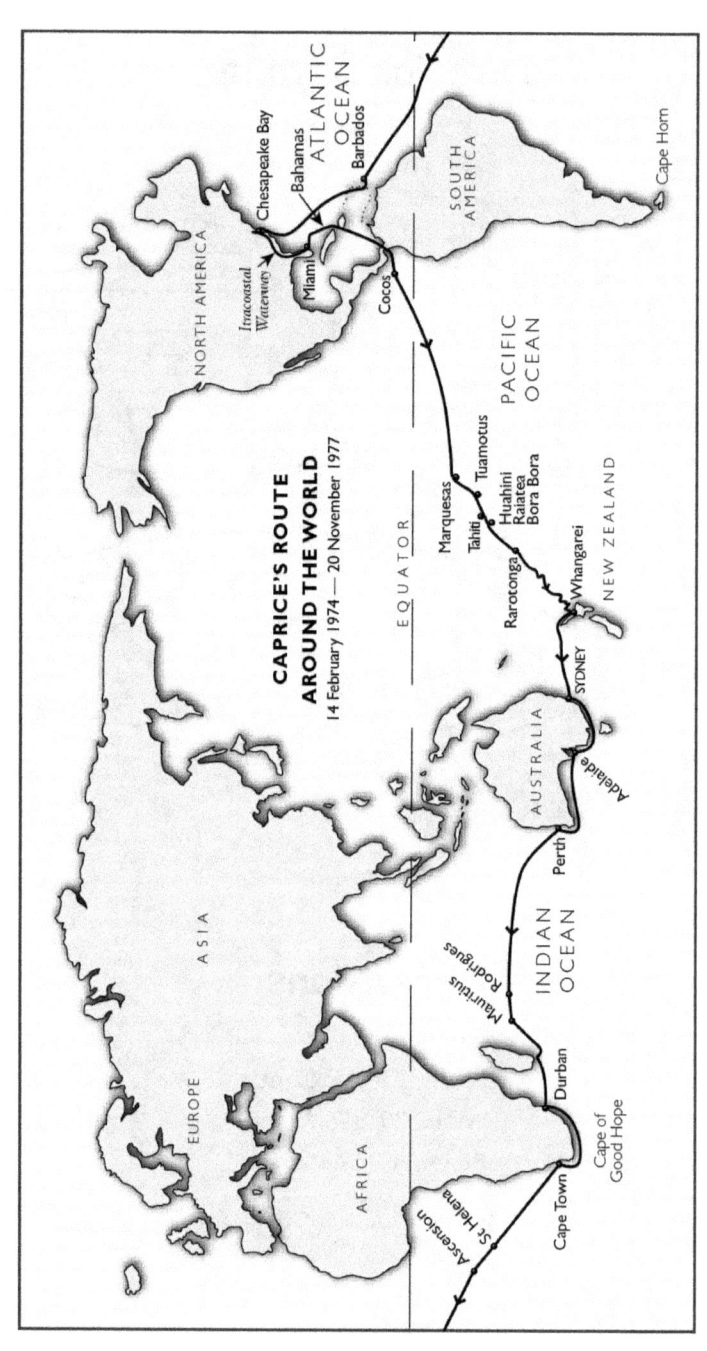

Part One:

12 Articles from Australian Sea Spray, Mar.-Aug. 1978

Jan Mitchell

1 The Shakedown Cruise

My husband and I have just completed a circumnavigation. We set off from Sydney in February 1974 and returned in November 1977, so we were away for three years and nine months. When we left, our only responsibilities were to ourselves and *Caprice*. By the time we returned, we had become a family; our son was two years old and I was six months pregnant.

Caprice is a fibreglass Top Hat sloop, LOA 25', built and launched in Sydney in 1969. We were not her original owners. How did we come to buy *Caprice* and why did we sail her around the world?

To ask a cruising sailor why he must sail the oceans is like asking a mountaineer why he climbs. When Ian is faced with the question, "What made you do it?' he just stares back blankly at the enquirer. For him, to be sailing his boat is to be alive. Any other existence is only half living or less.

The dream of sailing his own boat across oceans was born when he was twelve years old and chanced to read Bill Howell's *White Cliffs to Coral Reefs*, but it remained only a dream for the next twelve years. His parents did not live near the sea. He knew no one who owned or sailed a boat. But that did not stop him from reading every cruising book upon which he could lay his hands, teaching himself celestial navigation and while still in high school, starting to build a "Bluebird" in the backyard. However, when his parents moved house, he had to abandon the building project and the dream was submerged while he spent the next few years at Sydney University acquiring a degree in Civil Engineering.

Ian is, by nature, somewhat introverted, so that joining a yacht club, pushing himself forward to meet sailing people or gaining experience by crewing on other people's boats were approaches he could not consider. He wanted his own boat or nothing.

Then fate took a hand. One morning, while riding to work on his motorcycle, Ian was involved in an accident with a car. At an intersection, a car driver chose to flout several traffic rules.

In so doing, the car wiped out the motorcycle. Ian's crash helmet was smashed and he received head injuries, but with a policeman as witness, the insurance company paid up a considerable amount of compensation. Ian does not particularly recommend this method of gaining capital, but for him it, was a lifesaver. The money gave him an escape route from the drudgery of suburban living and career.

We had been acquaintances for several years, but it was not until a few months after the accident that we fell in love. When I heard about the insurance money, I insisted it be set aside to buy Ian's yacht and his dream of a circumnavigation began to acquire reality. Initially, I saw no part of this dream involving me. I was in Sydney only temporarily, studying for a Master's degree and in so doing, delaying my commitment to the New Zealand Department of Education for a further year of teaching.

However, as the year drew to a close, our relationship was closer than ever. The notion of leaving Ian and returning to New Zealand became inconceivable. I didn't know whether I wanted to go sailing. After all, I'd never even set foot on a sailing boat of any kind, but I did want to help Ian fulfil his dream.

Moreover, I'd always longed to travel. With the knowledge that Ian would sail whether I went with him or not, we married. A period of saving hard and looking for a boat began. In the meantime, Ian tried to build up my enthusiasm by giving me cruising books to read. Slowly, I began to learn the lingo, to recognise the difference between sloops, ketches and schooners, yet incredibly, neither of us had ever been sailing.

Hearing of our plans, a friend of a friend invited us to become acquainted with the realities of boat ownership. We spent a whole day helping scrape sand and paint his yacht. In return, the next weekend, he took us for a day sail in Sydney Harbour.

A few weeks later, Ian tried applying his theoretical knowledge to sailing a hired Mirror dinghy. He came home wet, cold but exuberant.

We began to spend our weekends at boatyards and marinas looking at all the yachts for sale at prices within our range. I found them depressingly claustrophobic. The interiors were dark, dingy and ill-planned. Frequently there was insufficient headroom for me – a mere five foot and two inches. I didn't know enough about boats to be able to imagine living aboard one of these after it had been cleaned up, given a coat of white paint and some gaily patterned curtains and cushions. The majority of these yachts had been used solely for racing. They'd never been cruising nor even lived in.

It was not surprising that I over-reacted when we found a 33' steel sloop with a bright airy interior, a large galley and a roomy double bunk. Here at last was a boat in which I felt comfortable standing or sitting. I didn't have to rush outside to breath after five minutes. It was like being in a caravan. Little did I realize that one does not go to sea in a floating caravan. Buoyed up by my enthusiasm, Ian minimised the number of alterations which would have to be made for *Jenny II* to become deep- seaworthy, and we bought her.

Fourteen months of very hard labour followed, during which time we learned a lot from our mistakes. However, it was obvious that even if we spent every minute of our spare time working on the boat, it would be another two years at least before she would be ready for cruising. One evening, Ian came home and announced that he'd put *Jenny II* up for sale. At first, I was very disappointed, but when she was sold, it was as though an enormous weight had lifted from our shoulders.

Next, we studied the designs of all the production yachts 24'- 30' long available on the east coast, trying to decide on the features which would best suit our requirements. Fed up with the maintenance problems of steel, we turned to fibreglass, but visits aboard many of those for sale in Sydney soon eliminated them from our choice range. They were of light displacement, had inadequate fuel and water tank space and the interiors were cluttered with bunks. Obviously they were not designed for long distance cruising, despite their manufacturers' claims. Rare indeed is the yacht which can satisfactorily meet the needs of both cruising and racing sailors without compromise.

Of all the boats we looked at, we soon came to the conclusion that the Top Hat design suited our needs best. She races well when unladen, but has the displacement to be still manageable when she is laden 6" down on her waterline marks. There is full head-room and ample stowage for food, water and fuel.

One Sunday morning, we were gazing at a Top Hat tied up at a marina. By coincidence, the owners arrived ready to go sailing and noticing our envy, invited us to accompany them. After several hours under sail in Pittwater and the swells of Broken Bay, I was not seasick! That clinched the decision for me and Ian was happy with the yacht's sailing characteristics. All we had to do was find a second hand Top Hat in good condition.

We could not believe our good fortune when, only a week or so later, we discovered one that had not even been advertised. As soon as we stepped aboard, I knew that we'd found our boat. It took but two days to complete the deal and she was truly ours.

Next, we had to learn to sail. Our few attempts to sail *Jenny II* had come close to minor catastrophes. By comparison, *Caprice* obviously wanted to show us how easy it could be. She was docile and patient with us, so that after three day-sails, we decided to take her further afield. We needed to gain some experience in practical navigation, night sailing, using self-steering and to learn what interior alterations would add to our comfort and safety.

I was working at Macquarie University, so the August - September students' vacation was the only time before Christmas that I could possibly get leave. Ian arranged for leave at the same time and we frantically made our preparations for a shakedown cruise to Lord Howe Island.

We ordered a trysail to complete the sail wardrobe, the cheapest available self-steering vane (the QME). Charts, fuel, food and water were stowed, and on the first morning of our vacation, we dropped our mooring lines and motored up Pittwater in the stillness of early morning.

Seasickness was still a problem I had to reckon with. We had to find out whether or not I would eventually get over it. Ian, on the other hand, had not once suffered from mal de mer. Using land-lubberly logic, I decided I that I'd better have some food in in my stomach on which to be sick.

Ian releases the mooring

Not knowing how long it might be before I would be capable of preparing another meal for Ian, I thought he should have a high-protein, cooked breakfast, and I'd better get the meal before we left sheltered waters. I cooked and served a six egg omelette with kippered herrings. As if that were not invitation enough for sea-sickness, I neglected to clean up the dishes immediately, even leaving the empty kipper can in the sink!

Before long, we were heading seawards with a moderate swell on our stern. The sea-sickness tablets had no hope of coping with my fishy breakfast and the latter soon joined the ocean waves. Despite my miseries, I was comforted an hour or so later to find that Ian was not immune to this weakness and he too was heaving heartily over the railing. Later, between bouts of sickness, he gallantly cleared away the remains of that never to be forgotten breakfast. To this day, neither of us can face kippered herrings in tomato sauce.

At first with full sail, the self-steering worked quite well, but later in the day, the wind strengthened and the mainsail had to come down. By evening, we were quite tired and weak with seasickness.

Having seen no ships for several hours and (wrongly we later found out) believing ourselves relatively clear of the coastal shipping lane, we lowered the jib, lashed the tiller to leeward, then retired below to the warmth of our bunks where we could be sick in comfort, soon to doze.

A few hours before dawn, I awoke, startled by bright lights shining in the starboard windows. Leaping up, I shouted out, 'Quick, start the engine! There's a town! We've drifted ashore!'

However, this was no town, but a large ship alongside, spotlight glaring at us. They slowly circled us, flashing Morse at a bamboozling rate. The ship edged in closer and someone shouted across to us. I waved madly and shouted back, 'We're okay, thanks' then subsided into giggles of nervous relief before being sick again. We were amazed that our little fibreglass yacht had been seen since, at that time, we carried no radar reflector.

We raised the jib and set an easterly course before a choppy sea and an increasing swell. Ian tried to take his first ever sextant sight that morning, but our general weakness and the choppy conditions made it very difficult. I discovered some glucose on board and managed to concoct a hot drink of milo, glucose and canned milk.

It was one of the most appreciated "meals" I've ever prepared. Soon we were feeling a little stronger. But not for long; the sea had become more regular, so we'd set the self-steering again and were both below resting when *Caprice* lurched violently as she slid down a wave. Ian was hurtled across the cabin on top of me, his forehead smashing against my mouth so that my teeth cut into my lower lip. The incident made us both sick again, although in general, our seasickness was waning.

That night, the wind increased and we sailed under storm jib, foolishly keeping the self-steering on despite an uneven course. The loom of Newcastle and an occasional ship could be seen in the distance. The weather continued to deteriorate the following day, our third at sea. Waves broke over the sides of the cockpit on several occasions and inevitably, water came below. Once, the yacht was knocked flat, the mast dipping into the water and again, I broke Ian's fall. This time however, my presence prevented his being thrown overboard.

The self-drainers in the cockpit could not cope with so much water, so we bailed furiously by bucket to allow the stern to rise again. Most of the books, assorted equipment and sextant stowed in the cabin shelves landed on the floor in a sodden heap. Stoically, I replaced them all, wiped up the floor and hunted for a rope to keep tied round my waist. We had only one proper harness on board at that time and Ian needed it for deck-work.

Late that evening, we set the self-steering again while we tried to get some rest. A few hours later, we were rudely awakened by a sudden lurch and what sounded like a gunshot. This time, we had really overtaxed our steering gear, and the lines had snapped, at the same time breaking the transmitter aerial which was attached to the starboard backstay.

We took over hand steering again, but this time, the weather deteriorated so badly that we were shooting dangerously down large waves at more than eight knots. The storm jib had to come in, but I didn't have the strength to hold the tiller. Instead I donned the safety-harness and crawled forward onto the wildly pitching foredeck in the stormy darkness. Although separated by only twenty feet, we could neither see nor hear the other, so it was with great relief to us both that I returned to the cockpit with the sail.

In trepidation, we laid *Caprice* broadside to the waves and wondered as she rose buoyantly with them. It worked just the way the books said! The motion was not at all comfortable and our morale was so low that we still feared being swamped. We retired to our bunks still wearing our saturated foul weather gear. On top, I strapped my life jacket. Ian's comment that, "it only prolongs the agony" didn't help.

We remained laid to for 24 hours, using the respite for battery charging, fixing the broken steering lines and mending a small tear in the storm jib. Ian practised with the sextant, taking a series of sights, then graphed them in order to eliminate any inconsistencies. By late afternoon, the sky had cleared, the wind dropped but illogically, the sea seemed to have eased only in the distance. The waves in our immediate vicinity appeared to have lessened hardly at all. We decided to move and to our amazement, the sea conditions did improve rapidly. Later, when we checked our position on a more up-to-date chart, we found that it showed a large seamount in that area.

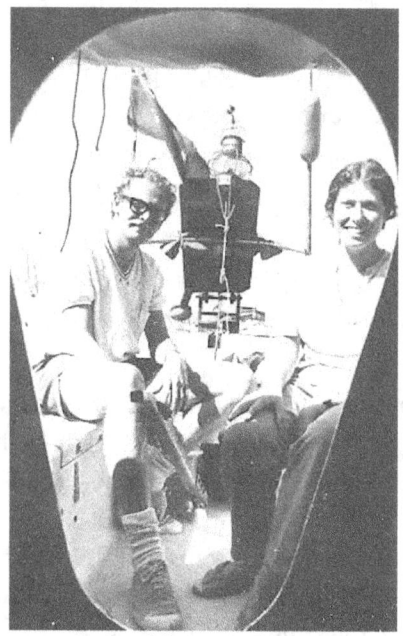

Ian and Jan steer by hand

For the next two days, we had mild, pleasant sailing. We were even becalmed for some hours, during which time Ian dived overboard into crystal clear water to remove a rope from round the propeller. On the morning of our seventh day at sea, we first sighted Lord Howe Island. In increasingly light conditions, we edged closer to the island and wary of coming too close to land at night without navigating lighting, we lay to, planning to make the difficult entry the following morning.

2 The Voyage Becomes a Nightmare

Seasickness was still a problem I had to reckon with. We had to find out whether or not I would eventually get over it. The night was dark, overcast and moonless. We strained our ears and eyes for signs of the island, fearing an onshore drift. Imagine our disgust when morning dawned we found Lord Howe almost out of sight. A current had taken us at least twenty miles to the south east. Whilst there had been only a light breeze during the night, the wind now began to brisk up from the north-west, directly in our faces. We started to beat back, using motor as well as sail, but our little yacht was no match against wind, current and seas. By afternoon, our progress had slowed to less than two knots through the water.

We estimated our position to be about ten miles south of Ball's Pyramid. In great despondency, we concluded that we had to turn back as we had only a further eight days in which to return to Sydney. Despite the few days of good weather, Ian was becoming physically and mentally exhausted. We had no winch for the wire mainsail halyard and Ian's hands were becoming raw with hauling on the wire. The salt encrusted boltrope was sticking in the mast track, so that on occasions, it took almost an hour to raise or lower the sail.

That night, the weather was ferocious. Wind and spray lashed our faces. Wave tops lopped into the cockpit and squall after black squall whipped us. Lightning bruised the sky purple, green and yellow. I huddled in my corner of the cockpit, whimpering in between thunder claps that I didn't want to die yet. Never have I been in the midst of a more terrifying electrical storm. I was sure the mast would be struck because we had no lightning conductor. Although we had the new trysail on board, we were reluctant to try setting it for the first time in such bad conditions, especially as *Caprice* was not at that time fitted with a proper topping lift. So under storm jib and double reefed main, we tried heaving to in the manner the books recommended. It worked and we slept.

In the morning, Lord Howe was only just visible nearly forty miles to the north. We set course for home.

Increasingly, we came to believe that there was a conspiracy afoot to prevent us reaching our destination, at the same time producing every kind of sailing condition imaginable. The weather eased until we were in a dead calm. In the early hours of our tenth day at sea, we set sail again in a light breeze. Within fifteen hours, we had raised and lowered every sail in the locker (except the spinnaker which we did not yet know how to use), moving from complete calm to full gale and electrical storm.

This time, the wave tops seemed to reach as high as our mast. When I stood in the cockpit and held the wind indicator at boom level, it registered 40 knots! The sky reflected our mood grey, overcast and miserable. I was severely seasick again for two and a half days. Ian struggled at the tiller for hours, fighting every wave, but we made very little progress westwards. Despondently, we lay to at nights.

Five days after we had turned back from Lord Howe, the weather cleared sufficiently for us to take sights again. We were astonished to find that our position was still more than 300 miles from Sydney. In fact we were over 100 miles due north of our last known position! At every set-back, I prayed regularly and fervently to God that if only He would let me back on land, I would never go to sea again. I became firmly convinced that man was foolish to tackle the oceans, which were not his element. Harbour sailing was okay, but the open sea was madness, I believed.

We were both losing a lot of weight, but Ian in particular was getting very thin and easily exhausted. Much of this was due to dehydration. The water in the main tank was growing algae and tasted quite bad. We had nothing with which to chlorinate it and nor had we brought much else in the way of drinks. Even after boiling the water, I was unable to keep it down. The salt spray on our faces increased our thirst as we licked dry cracked lips.

'Oh, for a long cool drink!' I recorded in my diary on our fourteenth day.

With nightfall, the wind came in on the starboard quarter, and later in the evening, we sighted a light which we optimistically guessed to be Smokey Cape just north of Newcastle.

Wild with enthusiasm at being close to land again, I took the tiller and set course for that light. For the rest of the night, *Caprice* galloped over those waves at close to six knots. I rode her every inch of the way. The sky was clear and moonlit and bio- luminescence surged by the hull.

Soon, town lights appeared. Could it be Newcastle? I asked myself hopefully. In the half light of dawn, we passed through the shipping channels, sighting two ships and altering course to avoid collision with a third. The early morning haze began to clear and in horror, I realized that not only were we close enough to the shore for me to clearly see the breakers on the beach, but there was a rocky islet several hundred yards ahead. I called Ian from his bunk, requesting a decision as to which way I should tack.

'Give me another half-hour's sleep, and then I'll decide,' came his sleepy reply. However, he rose smartly enough when I mentioned the breakers on the beach.

Soon we were sailing southwards, parallel to the coast. Armed with binoculars and the sailing directions, we scanned the coastline for landmarks to help identify our position. Such are the powers of self-delusion and optimism, we believed ourselves to be off Three Capes just north of Broken Bay. Ian even declared that he could see North Head through the binoculars. Our delusions were shattered when we were able to take a sight and realized that the town lights viewed earlier that morning were of Coolangatta on the Queensland/N.S.W. border.

This position was confirmed about midday when, still hugging the coast, we passed by Cape Byron with its distinctive light structure. We had visited the cape by land two years previously. It was unmistakable.

As we rounded the cape, the wind began to freshen from the north again. Although dressed only in her storm sails *Caprice* was soon racing down the waves at more than eight knots.

Under bare poles, our speed was reduced to four knots. We continued steering south until we sighted Ballina, but we didn't dare seek shelter there since we had no chart and there is a bar across the river. So we altered course seawards, cutting across the waves and shipping channels at close to five knots with no sail set. At first light, the hill behind Ballina was just visible.

Any attempts at sailing were soon thwarted by worsening conditions, so we hove to in yet another full gale under clear skies!

Wary of currents by now, Ian attempted to take sights in order to check our drift. The position lines showed us to be about 50 miles S.E. of Cape Byron. We remained hove to all night, setting sail very early on the morning of our 17th day at sea.

Near midday, we were puzzled to notice a heavy haze over the land, a city haze. Ian took sights at both noon and 3.00p.m. The seas had calmed right down and he had no difficulty in getting good readings. After much muttering and re-checking of his figures, he declared that our position was now 40 miles east of Newcastle! How could this be? Newcastle lies some 300 miles south of Cape Byron and we had logged less than 40 miles since our sights the previous day.

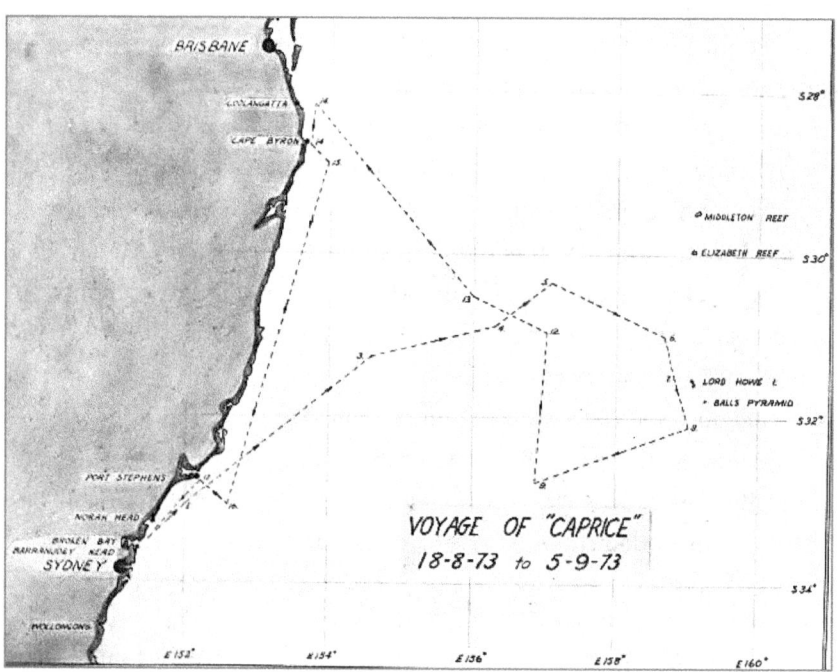

We were at the mercy of the current

Yet, there was the city haze to the west. My pulse was quickening, so I tried not to become too hopeful. We were at the mercy of the elements and I'd learned by then not to trust them. If that haze on the horizon were Sydney or Newcastle, we should see the loom of their lights at nightfall. That would confirm our position, we decided.

Now we were really fearful of the coastal current. If it could carry us over 200 miles in 24 hours against a southerly gale, it might sweep us right past Sydney. We set a north westerly course for Port Stephens in the hope of countering any southerly drift.

The loom of the city lights did not appear until 3.00 a.m., by which time we had almost convinced ourselves that we were hopelessly lost. Before long, we also picked up the flash of a lighthouse, then spent a couple of hours trying to work out which it could be.

Our 1957 sailing directions indicated no such light between Melbourne and Brisbane. Later, our suspicions that all the lights had been changed were confirmed. Once again, we made our land-fall under the shadow of a lighthouse in the first light of dawn. But where were we?

Had the current carried us south again? Were these hills to the north or south of Wollongong? I had almost convinced Ian that we should turn north when, as the sun rose, we sighted a fishing boat. Deciding to risk our dignity, we started the engine and hastened after them.

The fishermen were almost speechless when they heard Ian's question, then one man, recovering from his surprise, waved his arm towards the lighthouse, "Port Stephen's light!" Where on earth else did we think we were, his tone implied.

We thanked him and moved away before we should foul their trawl nets. For the first time in the voyage, we had set a course and made landfall at the intended place.

It was pleasant sailing that fine sunny morning and in the freshening breeze, we swept across the Newcastle Bight under storm jib. Norah Head was within sight late that afternoon when the wind dropped considerably. I decided to heat some soup for our evening meal before we increased sail.

While we were eating, two banks of heavy black cloud approached. Despite the warning signals, we were unprepared for a southerly buster this early in the year. We estimated the first gust of wind to be about 50 knots. It heeled us over to 60° and hurtled us towards the coast, the storm jib tipping the wave tops. With much effort, we managed to turn *Caprice* seawards, then Ian crawled up the slippery, sloping deck to lower the sail, while I thanked our lucky stars that he hadn't raised the genoa a half hour earlier.

Just where would we find ourselves at the end of this gale, I wondered bitterly, when we are so close to home. However, in true southerly buster fashion, the storm soon blew over and we were on our way again, still within sight of the coastal lights. It had been quite enough to revive all my fears that we would never get home. Exhausted as we were after 18 harrowing days, we felt unable to relax our vigilance for a moment.

Against a head wind, we tacked for several hours to clear Three Capes before reaching the entrance of Broken Bay. I was unable to relax sufficiently to go to bed; instead, I sat up in my waterproof gear, dozing uncomfortably. At approximately 3.30 a.m., we tried to make our way in under Barrenjoey Lighthouse, but the night was so dark and moonless, we pulled back at the last moment and spent three bitterly cold hours tacking back and forth just outside the bay.

I searched the lockers for our last cans of food to heat. Even spaghetti sauce without any spaghetti was appreciated. We resorted to stamping our feet and clapping our hands to keep the circulation going. There was not a lot of wind, yet it was the coldest night we had experienced at sea.

When the sky began to lighten, we sailed in past Barrenjoey Head. In the half light of dawn, the land was wreathed in a mysterious mistiness, the sea breathless. I began to believe I must be having hallucinations while drowning. This could not be Broken Bay! It had to be more of the Kafkaesque plot to disorientate us. Yet, there stood Barrenjoey, its light 'winking' at us over the port bow.

Soon the lights of Sydney's northern beach suburbs were extinguished and the pre-dawn chill was dissipating. Slowly, we tacked in towards the land beyond the headland. Distance was maddeningly distorted so that Barrenjoey joined with the landscape of the Hawkesbury River, and what we knew should be Lion Island merged into the river bank behind it. The entrance to Pittwater seemed to have disappeared, but as we approached, miraculously it opened up for us. This was like a dream. The Broken Bay we knew with its cross swell and waves was scarcely rippled in the light breeze.

Soon we were gliding noiselessly down Pittwater, the water so still that the hills, trees and houses were clearly reflected in it. With the big genoa set, we just had steerage way. The spell was suddenly broken by the approach of two fishing boats out of Careel Bay. The realization that our ordeal was really over slowly filtered into our tired brains, so that we began to make ready to tie up at our marina berth, which we had so casually left 18 days before.

Half an hour later, we stepped ashore and nearly fell off the other side of the jetty. I had lost so much weight I had to hold onto my jeans to prevent their falling about my ankles. While stowing gear and preparing to leave the boat, Ian came close to falling overboard. Everything was much too still!.

It wasn't until we phoned our respective places of employment (being three days overdue in reporting back to work) and Ian's mother that we found out that Air Sea Rescue had been alerted we were missing and were planning to initiate a shipping alert for us the following day.

By midday, we were home in our flat, showered and asleep in bed. We didn't even wait to eat first. It was not until after midnight that I awoke and seeing street lights through the window, yelled to Ian that we were being driven ashore.

Next, I climbed out of bed and peering through the window, assured him we'd better do something fast because it was certainly Curl Curl beach that I could see. A few minutes later, Ian had stilled my panic and we were both fast asleep again.

The next night, it was Ian's turn for nightmares. When the garbage-eating monster truck came clanking down the street, he sat bolt upright, clutching me.

'It's all right, we're home,' I reassured him, only to be assailed by doubts myself a few seconds later.

Both of us had difficulty with our sense of balance for several days. The only explanation we can offer for these reactions is the effects of dehydration, from which both of us were suffering quite severely. Five days after our return, I was still 10 lbs under my normal weight and Ian had lost 12 lbs.

Within a day or so of our return, Ian was making lists of alterations to be made to *Caprice*. He also had a list of food-stuffs (mainly quick energy carbohydrate snacks) he felt should be among the stores. Obviously, he had not found our experiences quite as nightmarish as I had.

As he recovered from his exhaustion, he began to look upon this voyage as a lesson for future voyages. Meanwhile, I was still declaring vehemently that I'd never sail again outside the heads.

Then, a month earlier than I expected, the professor called me into his office; Did I or did I not wish to renew my contract for the following academic year?

'How long do I have to make up my mind?' I asked.

'I need to know now,' he replied. 'We're advertising vacancies earlier this year.'

I stared at him dumbfounded. What could I say?

3 My Big Decision

An image of Ian sailing off alone flooded into my mind, with me left behind hungering for news of his safety. I knew I couldn't do it that way. Important as my academic career seemed at that time, I knew my relationship with Ian was more important to me.

'I'm going,' I blurted to the professor. With that short statement, I gave away my job, my chance of promotion the following year, my research plans.

Once the decision had been made, I set about planning my share of the preparations. I made careful calculations of how many cans could be stored in the lockers then translated this into our food needs. End of year marking, counselling and student assessment filled an ever diminishing part of my life as more and more evenings were spent helping Ian with fitting bolt-down lids to the forward lockers, varnishing the timber Q.M.E. self-steering and the new chart table, painting lockers, making canvas lee-cloths and canvas bags for stowage of clothing. I seemed to spend more time in hardware and camping stores than at the university.

Hours were passed on the telephone trying to find a reasonable insurance cover for *Caprice* (I didn't succeed), finding out where various plastic fittings and containers were available and establishing that the plastic cans we intended to use for extra fuel storage were made of polyethylene. Then there were the inevitable trips to and from the sail-makers and chart agencies.

One of the most memorable incidents which took place at this time was the transportation of the chart table and drawer frames out to *Caprice*. We still had no transport other than our motorcycles, so I climbed onto the pillion seat of Ian's Honda 250, he tied the chart-table to my back, then slowly drove the 15 km to Newport. We had not progressed very far along Pittwater Rd. when a traffic officer passed us.

He stared in astonishment, then stopped several hundred metres ahead. As we trundled past him, he was still shaking his head. Obviously, he thought he should book us for something, but he didn't seem to know quite what.

Not very much further on, we got a puncture. Carefully, Ian unloaded me and the chart table onto the grass verge, then he set about mending the puncture. Eventually, we loaded up again, and this time, reached the boat yard without further incident.

During January, the mountain of provisions stacked in the corner of the laundry/basement continued to grow. I spent days varnishing all the cans to protect them from rust, since we'd discovered that in a small boat, it is impossible not to bring water inside on foul weather suits and sails. After I'd assured Ian that I could fit all this food into the boat and there would still be space for us to sleep, he turned his concern to the weight of it all. He was still sceptical when I assured him I could keep it under 225 kg. How we would have laughed had we been able to see ourselves loading up later in the voyage. From Papéètè, we set off carrying 25 kg of milk powder alone, for by then, our baby, Jamie, was a milk hungry 20 months old.

Another concern for which I took major responsibility was organizing medical stores. I read the appendices of many cruising books and from that and our own personal needs, tried to make a list for ourselves. We were not adept at first aid, and I wondered just how well we would cope in a real medical emergency. I told myself (and Ian) that was the reason for keeping the old double side band transmitter which was already installed in *Caprice* when we bought her. Somewhere I must have read a story of an amateur conducting an operation as he followed instructions transmitted by a doctor.

Despite the experiences of our Lord Howe trip, I had not yet come to terms with the reality that at sea we had to be completely self-dependent.

We didn't approach Ian's brother, a G.P., for a surgical kit because we felt unsure that he, with no sailing experience, could envisage our possible needs, especially when we ourselves were unsure of our capabilities in an emergency. Instead, we accepted from a veterinary friend, a gift of forceps, scissors, suture materials, local anaesthetic, syringes and some antibiotics. We reached Durban before we found time to attend even a basic St. John's Ambulance course in first aid.

Uncertain of our ability to sail even as far as Western Australia, it seemed strange to be arranging for passports, visas to South Africa and vaccinations. But we'd made so many decisions that we had to assume we were going to succeed. After several visits to the doctor, we were finally protected against smallpox, cholera, typhoid and yellow fever.

A week after the smallpox vaccination 'took', I thought I was going to die. The first reaction set in while I was doing the Saturday morning shopping. An hour later, I literally crawled up the stairs and into bed beside Ian who had succumbed the previous day. For two days, we scarcely moved except to compare the height of our fevers.

Cleaning out the algae from the water tank was an important task if we were to avoid a repetition of our dehydration during the shakedown cruise. We obtained a strong algaecide which we left in the filled tank for several days before we pumped it out and flushed the tank several times with fresh water.

When the aluminium parts of the galley pump disintegrated, we wondered if we hadn't over done it. Although the alga was gone, the plastic flavour remained. It was during our stop-over in Western Australia that we finally came to terms with the water problem.

Assuming that the resin used in the tank was the cause of the plastic flavour, Ian cut out the floor which forms the top of the water tank and using *dynel* with epoxy resin, re-lined the inner surface.

Only after this extensive job had been completed did I realize that the water improved in flavour only after the first few strokes of the pump. We looked at the line leading from the tank to the pump. It was made from regular plastic garden hose! After that had been replaced with polythene drinking water hose and we began using swimming pool chlorine to prevent algae growth, we had no more problems. However, we did also take the precaution of carrying a minimum of two twenty litre jerry cans of water in case the main supply became contaminated.

Towards the end of January the pace became hectic. We packed all our possessions, then hired a truck for two days. The truck refused to go up the steep incline of the drive, so everything had to be carried down to street level. There, firstly we loaded the food stores and drove to the boat yard where every box had to be carried down steep wooden stairs before it could be put on a trolley and wheeled the length of the jetty to *Caprice*.

Even I began to have doubts about my calculations when I saw the size of the pile. Never the less, I diligently took the boxes as Ian passed them down the fore-hatch and I began stowing. Finally, I packed in all but two dozen cans, and triumphantly told Ian he needn't have worried.

As we prepared to leave, we checked the waterline. Despite the fact we'd raised the boot-topping by 5 cm the last time *Caprice* was slipped, it was now below the water. Although I'd pulled a muscle in my back and Ian had developed his old favourite of tendonitis in the knee, there was no respite. We had to go home and reload the truck ready for the drive down to Bowral the next morning.

We stored our belongings safely with Ian's mother, staying the night before driving back to Sydney. At our departure, my mother-in-law was tearfully reluctant to be reassured by my assertion that we would return safely. At the time, this belief came to me very strongly. At various stages of our voyage, I was to think back to that moment and wonder whether our luck really would hold until we were home again.

Back in Sydney, we packed the truck with yet another load of gear which we raced out to the boat. As our proposed departure date neared, Ian frantically studied the wiring circuits in the engine manual, trying to discover why the engine lacked power. Since the electrics are very complicated; he was sure the fault lay there. Eventually, he gave up. Already we had seen too many people postpone their departures because everything was not perfectly ready. Once the essentials for safety have been completed, it is better to set a date and stick to it as closely as the weather permits.

Soon, all that remained was to clean up the house for the return of its owners, sell our motorcycles and say farewell to our friends.

At last, we moved aboard *Caprice*, where we spent our remaining few days in Pittwater completing odd jobs and awaiting favourable weather for the sail down the NSW coast.

Loading up for departure

4 Casting Off

We believe in early departures when commencing a voyage. At 8.35a.m., on Tuesday, 5th February, 1974 we waved goodbye to a friend working on another yacht, cast off our mooring lines and slowly edged out into the channel with the engine showing its usual grudging performance.

The sky was semi-overcast and the wind very light, making progress up Pittwater exceptionally slow, almost to the point that we were being carried only by the tide. A few power boats and motor cruisers disturbed the calm water which was thick with large jelly fish. We had never seen so many all grouped together. I gazed at them, fascinated by their slow pulsating movements until the *Sumlog* stopped its regular ticking. Obviously, a jelly fish had caught itself round the log's propeller. It didn't free itself until much later that day.

As we were passing Careel Bay, Keith Newlands, an acquaintance who moored near us, sailed his 40' wooden sloop out towards us. Keith was setting out on a single-handed cruise to Port Davey in S.W. Tasmania. We thought he had made his departure the previous afternoon when he slipped his moorings, but apparently he had anchored overnight near his home. We suspect that he had been waiting to see us on our way.

Together, we drifted out of Pittwater. Ian would have used the motor had Keith not been there. Perhaps he may have had the same thought. Instead, we almost became entangled with the International Soling Championships being held in Broken Bay that week.

The winds remained extremely light all day. Keith was lost from sight by 3.00 p.m., he hugging the coast while we tried to gain sea room and hopefully pick up some current. In the late afternoon, the breeze swung to the N.E. and strengthened, so we swopped our genoa for the working jib. A southerly had passed through the previous day so we had hopes of northerly winds for two or three days.

After my previous experience of sea-sickness, I had taken full precautions this time. Yet, despite dosing myself with *Marzine* for two days prior to departure and taking care with food, I still experienced a few hours queasiness.

After four hours of peaceful sleep the first night, I felt fine and consumed a hearty breakfast. But by midday, it became obvious that our northerly winds had been short lived and another southerly was on its way. As the sails were reefed, then eventually doused, our queasiness increased. *Caprice* lay to, rolling and rising to the waves while our stomachs also rolled and rose. All my doubts about my sailing capabilities began to reassert themselves. I regretted throwing away my job and had serious doubts about our ability to sail *Caprice* through Bass Strait without misadventure. With these thoughts in mind, I pressed Ian into trying to establish a schedule for radio contact with the shore. He made a contact that afternoon, but the other party failed to respond to the next call we arranged with them. Perhaps that was not surprising since Ian arranged that call for 2.00 a.m. the following morning. We did manage to contact a shore station the next day, but then gave up our efforts with radio. The batteries would soon have been flat. We lay to until late the next afternoon by which time we felt dubious about our position. There was no hope of a sextant sight, but the sighting of a naval vessel led us to hope that the current had drifted us to somewhere near Jervis Bay.

Feeling weak from seasickness, we despondently tacked back and forth into the coast, then back out to sea, making virtually no progress southward. That evening, as we neared the coast, the lights of a town appeared startlingly close. It was only the next morning that we identified our position when, to the north, we sighted the tall smoke-belching chimneys of Port Kembla's steel mills. It was not until Friday, our fourth day at sea, that we eventually, tacked our way round Cape Perpendicular.

The sea moderated at last, allowing *Caprice* a more steady motion. Once we were able to eat properly again, morale rose rapidly. Just before midnight, during my watch, we passed well clear of Jervis Bay, obviously being assisted by current. The lighthouse disappeared astern quite rapidly. It was a good night. We were making comfortable progress; there were no sail changes, no emergencies, no inquisitive ships and most important, we both managed to get several hours sleep. With the improvement in weather, the temperature rose to 25°c.

We had worn the same clothes through the three days of storm, so after shedding our heavy water-proofs, we were eager to bathe. The seawater temperature was rather chilly for washing in the cockpit, so we rejoiced in a warm sponge bath and a change of clothes. Warm, clean and comfortable and with the threat of seasickness gone, we began to relax and enjoy ourselves. The self- steering needed only an occasional helping hand.

That night, we picked up a strong current which we estimated at about seven knots. It carried us well clear of Montague Island and by midday on Sunday, our sixth day at sea, we had also passed Gabo Island and were heading into Bass Strait.

My reaction to the pleasant sailing conditions can be seen in my diary entry for that day: "And yet the weather still holds. This isn't sailing weather as we knew it en route to Lord Howe. Still, there's bound to be bad to come, so we shall enjoy the calm while we can."

Later the same day, we came dangerously close to causing ourselves serious trouble. It all began when Ian asked me to lead a line forward round the rail and back again. It was a hot, almost cloudless day, so I was wearing my floppy-brimmed sunhat in an effort to protect my nose and neck.

I was also wearing my safety harness and its rope was entangled with the sheet. To go forward, I had to disentangle the ropes by passing one over my head. Off came my sunhat and plopped into the water. So the fiasco began. Firstly, my safety line became tied round the mast, then I came close to knocking Ian overboard with my wild swinging of the boathook. By the time the sunhat was irretrievably drowning, we had tied ourselves into knots around jib sheets, boom preventers and my safety line. We felt very guilty about our inability to rescue a sunhat under ideal conditions. What were our own chances if one of us went overboard?

Late in the afternoon, the wind changed and strengthened on our stern, bringing with it a following sea with wind waves of two metres.

It was a cold, wet and tiring night with wave tops splashing down my neck and trickling inside my shirt. With the clouds obscuring the moon and stars, my reactions of disbelief in the beautiful weather, recorded in my diary only that morning, seemed justified. Sailing was a wet, uncomfortable, storm-ridden existence. I was thoroughly depressed. We were in the dreaded Bass Strait and I was sure conditions could only continue to worsen. Despite my pessimism, the wind eased during the next few hours and the weather cleared a little. Watches were spent scanning the horizon for ships' lights and oil rigs. Our morale rose as we sighted each rig near to where we estimated it should be.

During the day, we sighted land again and then in the evening, the setting sun brilliantly lit up the Seal Islands, making them appear much closer than they really were. It was a tense night we spent watching for lighthouses on the islands as well as for ships, the west-bound shipping channel being quite narrow until Wilson's Promontory.

The westerly winds forecast that morning sprang up during the night, and next morning found us still tacking near the Seal Islands. With no current to help us, it took a whole day to edge our way past the islands and finally clear Wilson's Promontory, the southernmost point of mainland Australia. The first hurdle of our southerly route was behind us.

The beauty of that late afternoon was spoiled by the arrival on board of several houseflies and a blowfly. In indignation, I swatted and sprayed them. One of the pleasures of cruising is to be free from flying pests while at sea. How dare they intrude! We continued to make good progress during the next three days, passing south of the entrance to Port Phillip then rounding Cape Otway without difficulty. We had logged over 650 sea miles.

The self-steering was taking its expected share of watches, allowing us time to read and get sufficient sleep, but we were wary about allowing ourselves to become too optimistic.

The QME Steering Vane moves the tiller

Our main water supply continued to bedevil us. Not only had the strong plastic flavour returned only a few days after filling the tank, wood chips were frequently jamming the pump. We began to wonder if the bulkhead separating the water tank from the bilge was disintegrating. Ian successfully dismantled and cleaned the pump at least twice before we reached Western Australia. We never found where those chips had come from. At least, despite the plastic flavour, the water had not started growing algae again.

On the 11th day out, we were becalmed for the first time. It was hot and humid. What appeared to be dead locusts drifted by us early in the morning. Later, a swarm of flies and other insects flew in. Since we were many miles out of the sight of land, this time I was even more indignant than before.

The oppressiveness made us suspect that an electrical storm was in the offing, especially since a strong southerly was forecast. However, neither the strong winds nor the heavy seas predicted materialized. The winds that night were variable and it didn't even rain. In the morning, the wind settled to blow steadily from the N.E. once again, allowing us to make steady progress.

Off Cape Jaffa later that day, we encountered a hazard which was not mentioned on our chart or pilot book: a fishing ground which we eventually estimated to be at least one square mile in area. We tried to skirt the nets and their coloured marker buoys, but not knowing the extent of the area, sailed over a number of nets. It was quite harrowing trying to dodge the buoyed edges of the nets and we were apprehensive that we would entangle our propeller.

From Cape Jaffa, we set a course to take us through the Backstairs Passage between Kangaroo Island and the mainland and so into the Gulf of St. Vincent. With a moderate wind astern, we had difficulty in getting the self-steering to hold *Caprice* on course, so we had to continue duty at the tiller. We made a good day's run at 5-6 knots, coming into the coast again at dusk.

We were uncertain how far north of west we'd come, but felt certain that soon we'd see the flash of the light marking Backstairs Passage. Believing ourselves to be south of the passage, we turned north. About 10.30 p.m. we found ourselves offshore of a town.

There are no towns on Kangaroo Island and there was still no sign of a lighthouse, so we decided to lie to until morning. At dawn, we were shocked to find how close we were to the cliffs and rocky islets off the shore. We would never have slept so well had we known.

After much deliberation over the Pilot Book coastal descriptions, we identified the town then set sail south towards the passage, the early morning breeze speeding us along the coast. Later, while we were breakfasting in the cockpit, a couple of dolphins came to investigate our boat. They were the first we had ever seen at sea.

A few hours later, we were sailing through the Backstairs Passage and by early afternoon, *Caprice* was making an excellent run up the coast towards Adelaide. Given the unreliable nature of our engine, we decided not to go on to the port of Adelaide itself, but to select one of the smaller anchorages a few miles south. We chose Port Noarlunga as being suitably close and protected. There must have been a current assisting us, for we reached Port Noarlunga at sunset. Unable to find the leading marks described in the Pilot Book, we were unwilling to risk taking *Caprice* through the reef, so we spent a fairly uncomfortable night anchored outside.

Next morning, Ian rowed the dinghy ashore where he set off in search of the local Council engineers. They seemed extraordinarily surprised that anyone should want to use their "port". After unsuccessfully trying to persuade Ian to go on to Adelaide, the engineer gave him a small chart of the bay. The beacons on the dunes had been removed long ago when the land was sub-divided for housing. No other boat had anchored there in ten years.

How proud we felt of ourselves. We had sailed from Sydney to South Australia in 14 days without serious mishap, even for the most part, in reasonable comfort. Following a thoroughly lazy and pleasant weekend with our friends and relatives in Adelaide, we returned to *Caprice*. As the car breasted the hill, we looked at each other in relief. There was our boat still swinging happily at anchor.

We never fail to experience that tightening of the chest in the few minutes preceding the moment we actually see that she is still there and afloat. Whilst I did some shopping, Ian laboured over the engine once more, to no avail.

We decided to wait until the tide clearly showed the break in the reef before venturing out. I stood on the bow trying to spot any rocks ahead while Ian experienced heart failure every time the engine faltered. We made it safely. My emotions that fine afternoon were somewhat mixed. There was relief at being out in the Gulf of St Vincent and knowing that by nightfall, we'd be clear of the land, a nagging anxiety that next time we needed the engine, it would fail us, pleasure in the ideal sailing conditions with a gently warming sun and kindly breeze, yet still the familiar trepidation experienced at the beginning of any passage. A few hours passed before queasiness set in. I had rather hoped that after only five days ashore, I might be spared the misery of seasickness. Although I was sick only once, we both had difficulty in getting any sleep. But what did it matter? We could sleep the next day. The sky was brilliant with stars and a new moon. The best possible time to start a passage is with the new moon, then, unless it is a very long ocean crossing, you have moonlight when you approach your landfall. Moreover, I find that watch-keeping on moonless nights tends to be depressing and therefore more tiring.

That first night, we crossed Investigator Strait. At noon, soon after passing to port of the Althorpe Islands, the wind dropped off almost entirely and did not pick up again until sundown. By midnight, the wind was sufficiently settled for the steering vane to cope, allowing us a few hours of welcome sleep. We sighted no ships and before morning, were well clear of the land. Queasiness was the only thing which marred the second morning. The weather was fine and warm, the favourable breeze constant. We washed and sunbathed in the cockpit, after which I did some laundry.

For five days, the silent helmsman dutifully kept us on course and *Caprice* made steady progress across the Great Australian Bight. Overcast skies, drizzle and, for me, intermittent seasickness were minor distractions from otherwise excellent progress. We read, ate and slept while *Caprice* sailed herself. Two days spent at the tiller were regarded as a welcome change.

Then the wind fell very light and Ian decided to experiment with setting the spinnaker. First, he re-read the "how to" sections of several sailing manuals, then, following the instructions, set the sail. However, it was getting it down again which worried us both, especially if there should be an unexpected squall. Fortunately, it did come down without mishap, except that Ian let go the halyard. Better the sail flying free than the spinnaker pole! With the spinnaker safely packed away again, we set the working sails on the opposite tack. I promptly became sea-sick again, the queasiness continuing for a full two days.

Once again to match my mood, the sky became overcast with occasional drizzle. When we didn't need to hand-steer, we lay in our bunks reading or dozing, getting up to look around the horizon every fifteen minutes. We saw only a half dozen ships during the twelve days of sailing from the Gulf of St. Vincent to Cape Leeuwin.

Cape Leeuwin was extremely kind to us. We had sighted the coast again about twenty four hours before, and sailed just within sight of land all day. That night, while I took the tiller, Ian went to sleep in the expectation that he would come on watch again before we rounded the cape. However, the current was fully as strong as indicated in the Pilot Book.

I was unaware of the notorious reputation of Leeuwin, so I merely noted our excellent progress with delight as we raced past the lighthouse that clear moonlit midnight. Before long, I was waking Ian for help in altering course to the north. Bleary-eyed, he came on deck and looked about for the light. It was only after seeing his expression when I pointed astern that I began to realize the dangers of such a strong current close to a rock-strewn coast. The drink I offered in celebration of a successful southern crossing was drunk in relief that our voyage had not ended on those rocks.

A moderate following sea enabled us to romp up the West Australian coast, but the swell was too high for taking sextant sights. We tried to get a position using the RDF (Radio Direction. Finder), but although it had been working before we left Sydney, now we were unable to derive a sensible or consistent reading from it. As a result, we sailed past Rottnest Island, sighting the light there to the S.E. at nightfall. We had to turn and beat into sea and weather, taking a further sixteen hours to reach Fremantle harbour.

We had intended to sail up the Swan River to Perth, where we thought we'd moor at a marina or yacht club. However, when we approached the first bridge, it dawned on us that we'd misinterpreted the Pilot Book. A "navigational arch" did not mean that the bridge opened! Since we could not proceed up the river, we tied alongside the tugboat jetty for the night and gratefully accepted the offer of hot showers.

The next morning, we were offered a mooring at the C.Y.C. of W.A. which is based at Rockingham at the southern end of Cockburn Sound. We sailed down to Rockingham that day, where we received a fine welcome and many offers of assistance. We stayed there for three months, awaiting the season for the Indian Ocean crossing.

Ian and Jan in the cockpit before departing Australian waters
Photo by Rockingham local news

5 Departing Australian Shores: The Indian Ocean

Ian awoke with a hangover. That day, half way through May, we left Western Australia for our first major ocean crossing. The previous evening, we had entertained the customs official and later been farewelled by members of the club. Another cruising couple dropped by in their dinghy to say a final goodbye.. I completed the stowage of last minute items. Then, all too suddenly, the sails were up and we were leaving our mooring. In farewell, a club member rang a bell from her waterfront garden.

With the realisation that we were actually leaving Australia, a spasm of fear swept over me. Ian had to snap at me to help him clear away lines and set the genoa properly. By the time we had sailed under the bridge which links Garden Island to the mainland, I had dried my eyes, but the knot in my stomach took several hours to disappear.

We set course to pass to the south of Rottnest Island. The magnetic anomaly in the vicinity of the island caused our compass to behave quite erratically as we sailed by a few miles closer than we'd intended. We swept along at six knots on a very calm sea with a light swell. I was slightly queasy for only an hour. What a difference it made to have lived aboard at the mooring in not so calm waters.

We were leaving Australia with less in savings than we'd anticipated. Casual work had been almost impossible to find. Ian had finally been offered the dirty task of cleaning out pressure vessels at the local oil refinery for very meagre pay by Australian standards. The position was available for only five weeks. I managed a mere five days of relief teaching at a local school. For the rest of our three months' stay, I occupied myself with touching up the varnish work, ordering stores and varnishing cans, making courtesy flags and searching for those innumerable simple items that are always so difficult to buy.

On our second day out, we saw our first Tropic Bird (the red-tailed variety), a sooty albatross and many Wilson's petrels. There were also lots of Portuguese Men of War floating by and Ian had heard dolphins during the night. Until then, we'd seen very little marine life. Having other living creatures about took the edge off the loneliness of suddenly being out at sea and heading away from Australia.

A red-tailed tropic bird

We decided to put to advantage the excellent weather for me to learn to use the sextant. Although I'd attended navigation classes in Sydney, the theory had passed over my head. I persuaded Ian to forget the geometry and teach me the practical aspects of taking and working a sight. I insisted he should write out a 'recipe'. Despite calm seas, my first attempts with the sextant were very erratic, but they gained in consistency as I practised.

For several days, the weather was variable, requiring frequent sail changes. During the short calm periods, we motored to keep the batteries charged.

Whilst at Rockingham, we had discovered that the engine fault was mechanical, not electrical. If the electrics had not been so complex, Ian may not have immediately looked for an electrical source to the problem. It turned out that an incorrect connection in the exhaust system had caused the exhaust to choke up until the pipe was almost totally blocked. No wonder we had very little power!

The RCA Dolphin engine electrics

On the fifth day, we set the twin running sails for the first time. In Fremantle, we had a new working jib made, exactly the same as the original one, especially for trade-wind conditions. However, we weren't yet in the trades. Soon we were back to working rig. The approach of a front brought brisk winds and high humidity then rain, overcast skies and squally conditions for a couple of days. The seas did not rise much though, so that *Caprice* made good progress, enabling us to log 600 sea miles for the first seven days.

After ten days at sea, we were out of touch with Australian broadcast radio during the day, but we'd had our first flying fish aboard and were sailing under the twin running sails again. Soon we were discovering the delights of trade wind sailing in tropical waters. The water was a warm 24°c and as we moved westwards, it increased to 25°c. The air temperature remained close to that of the water so we delighted in cockpit baths every day.

We celebrated my 28th birthday by eating in fine style. Smoked oysters, nuts, cheese and brandy-soaked plum pudding were on the menu with warm beer for lunch, while dinner featured Chinese spiced duck and noodles served with sweet and sour vegetables. For desert, we ate strawberries and cream followed by coffee and liqueur. Although most of the food had been canned, we felt we had dined regally. My birthday present was a course alteration to the west. We'd made sufficient northing, so from there on, we marched steadily westwards at 20°S.

The temperature at nights dropped only slightly and we were able to sleep without blankets. Watch-keeping at night became a pleasure. Dolphins zipped through the bow wave and under the hull, leaving sparkling trails of bio-luminescence. Although the stars in the tropical sky do not sparkle with the brilliance they have in southern waters, the sky is bright with the light of the planets and moon. Many times, we saw 'falling stars'. Undoubtedly, many were merely seabirds swooping, the moonlight glinting on their wing tips, but some must have been small particles from space burning up as they entered the earth's atmosphere.

After only three days under the twin sails, the mast fitting for one of the poles became badly bent, so we returned to setting one foresail and winging out the mainsail with a preventer on the boom. A few nights later, light conditions encouraged us to keep the spinnaker up.

In the early hours of the morning during my watch, there was a sharp crash. I looked up to see the spinnaker flying out of control. Within thirty seconds, Ian, who had been soundly asleep, was on the fore-deck wrestling with the flapping sail and flailing poles. I stayed at the tiller, holding *Caprice* before the wind. I expected that at any moment, Ian would receive a nasty blow from one of the poles.

To my surprise, suddenly everything was on deck and the danger was over. Only then did we find out what had happened. Ian had lashed blocks to the anchor cleat to take the down hauls from the spinnaker poles; but the lashing chafed through, allowing the poles to swing up suddenly, breaking one mast fitting and bending the other. That put an end to using the running sails or spinnaker.

Within two hours, the wind began to strengthen, bringing with it three days of dirty weather, two metre quartering seas, rain and enough wind to push *Caprice* along at 5 - 6 knots under the storm jib alone. Perhaps it was just as well we had been forced to bring in the spinnaker at the time we did.

During our spare time, we occupied ourselves mostly with writing up our journals and reading. I was trying to teach myself shorthand in the hope of qualifying for a short term office job in Durban, (I'd done a touch typing course before we left Sydney), whilst Ian tried to teach himself to play the harmonica. We also tried our luck at trolling a fishing line but, probably through our own incompetence, we didn't catch anything edible.

By the time we'd been at sea for 22 days, we began to feel ourselves to be in limbo. The sea miles rolled by effortlessly, not noticed until our position was marked on the chart. All those little crosses marching across the paper seemed quite unrelated to our progress.

The timeless quality of our lives was such that when we were becalmed one day, we just went to sleep. I awoke in time to notice a particularly beautiful sunset and went out on deck to photograph it. The shutter had just clicked when there was a noise like a horse snorting right behind me. I swung round to find a whale about the same size as *Caprice* staring at me. Soon, three more of about the same size surfaced.

Unfortunately, I'd just used the last shot on the film and by the time I'd loaded a new one, darkness had fallen. These were the first whales we'd seen at sea and having recently read the story of the Robinson family, whose yacht was sunk by a killer whale, I felt they were more than close enough. The following day, we saw several more whales of the same kind, though smaller.

After four weeks at sea averaging 100 sea miles per day, we were disappointed to find the trade winds disappear not just for a few hours, but for five days. Whenever there was a slight breeze, we raised sail, but made very little progress. When the wind did return, conditions were so brisk that we had to hand- steer.

At dawn on our 38th day at sea, we found the vague outline of Rodrigues Island visible on the western horizon. We had sailed 3,500 sea miles and found the island right over our bows. My faith in Ian's ability to navigate soared.

Ian taking a sextant sight at sea

The wind increased as we neared the island. We were closing with it more quickly than we'd anticipated. There was a frantic scramble to clear up dishes, ready flags and anchor, read and re-read the pilot book's instructions on how to negotiated the channel through the reef and reduce sail.

We entered the lagoon under sail, our mistrust of the engine lingering despite having found the fault. We took the narrower of the two passes because of the wind direction and it was decidedly hair-raising to have coral clearly visible through the translucent water so close to our hull. This was our first time sailing in coral waters and we were thoroughly nervous about it.

The anchor warp had no sooner run out and been belayed than a local boat arrived to greet us and escort *Caprice* to a mooring until we'd received customs, immigration and health clearance. The formalities over, we moved *Caprice* in alongside the town wharf where it appeared that half the town's people of Port Maturin had turned out to witness our arrival.

A very tall, good looking young man dressed in a black shirt and blue jeans turned out to be the harbour official, constable and self-appointed host to visiting yachties. He drove us to the telegraph station so that we could send telegrams to our ever anxious parents, then invited us to his home for showers later in the afternoon, when the water was turned on.

During the time of our visit, the island was suffering from a severe drought. The land is not sufficiently high to attract rain from the trade wind clouds as does its greener neighbour, Mauritius. Instead, Rodrigues relies upon cyclones. The previous season, none.

A lateen-rigged dugout sails out of Port Maturin

Consequently, there was also a food shortage and we saw many animals and poor people who were suffering from malnutrition. Seeing the drought conditions made our showers doubly luxurious. It was sheer bliss to get the salt washed out of my long hair after a whole month at sea. Later, we walked through the dusty streets of the small port, quickly stepping aside at the jangle of a bicycle bell or motorcycle horn. Most of the four- wheeled vehicles are government-owned Land Rovers.

The people, like those of Mauritius which governs the island, are a mixture of many races, but Creole, Indian, Chinese and some European predominate. Although the islands became British after the Napoleonic wars, bastardised French or Creole is still the patois. Officially, English and French are spoken, but few understand English.

During our stay, a never ending succession of people lined the jetty during daylight hours, endlessly staring, chattering, dreaming of the 'rest of the world' of which we were one of the few tangible representatives to impinge upon their quiet island existence.

Port Maturin, Rodrigues

On what appeared to us to be such an idyllic island, I believed the people ought to be more carefree than they appeared. They had little appreciation of the things for which we envied them, and longed to acquire the material goods of the 'outside'. We were asked many times about life in Australia, the immigration policy and told of relatives who had gone there. It was sad to be told again and again what poor quality were local products. When we were invited out in the evening, we were offered Australian made pretzels, potato crisps, cheese, biscuits and savouries. That we might prefer locally produced food did not enter their heads.

Contact with the rest of the world is limited to a six-seater aircraft which flies from Mauritius three times weekly, weather permitting, a monthly visit from an inter-island steamer which also visits the Seychelles and goes to Perth every few months to bring back flour and other Australian products. A few yachts call each season. We were the first that year.

We remained in Rodrigues for ten days, fast making friends with the hospitable islanders. We were driven across the island to see the new airport and taken on a picnic. A young fellow arranged the loan of motorcycles for us, the hire fee being that they should be filled with petrol on our return.

Ian was taken out fishing at the edge of the reef. Our laundry was done for us and we were given beautifully cooked meals. The less people have, it seems, the more they want to give. We were sad to leave these friendly people, but so early in our voyage, we were reluctant to linger too long in any one place.

The day we left, the wind was gusting to 40 knots at the weather station on the hill above Port Maturin. The pilot and the chief of police, who had befriended us, both tried to persuade us not to go. Ian knew that the conditions would be easier clear of the island, and was determined to go when he was ready.

Rodrigues officials farewell Caprice

The crowded pilot boat towed us through the narrow dredged channel into the lagoon where, to the accompaniment of toots, whistles and much waving, we raised sail, shot out of the reef through the wider western channel along with the tide and were soon heading towards Mauritius.

6 Meeting Other Cruising Folk

Soon after we were clear of Rodrigues, *Caprice* was running briskly downwind with only the storm jib set. At first, the sea was confused and conditions squally, so that the steering vane wouldn't cope and we had to hand steer through the night and all the next day.

Obviously, the brisk conditions didn't bring on any bouts of seasickness because my diary contains enthusiastic references to our change in diet. In Rodrigues, I bought some meat canned in the Republic of China. Stewed pork, roast goose and spiced duck made a very welcome change from stew or corned beef.

After three days at sea, we sighted the first of the small islands lying off Mauritius to the north. We kept our course north of all the land. This turned out to be a very wise precaution, for that night we discovered that all the small islands were unlit, even those shown on the chart to have lights.

In the dawn of the fourth day, we sailed down the west coast of the main island. Mauritius looked magnificent in the early morning light, with its dramatically jagged peaks and green slopes. About a mile outside the harbour entrance, we first noticed the oil slick. As we entered the harbour, the oil and floating garbage became thicker.

I raised the courtesy and quarantine flags as well as our Australian ensign, then Ian readied mooring lines, anchor and warp while we circled about, awaiting the pilot boat which the Pilot Book assured us was obligatory for "ALL vessels entering Port Louis". Eventually, one came by and we were asked whether we had an engine. It became obvious the "all vessels" did not include us.

However, rather than get into difficulties between languages explaining where we should tie up, they threw us a line and towed *Caprice* in alongside a broad-beamed steel ketch bearing the American colours.

Before any officials appeared, we found people clambering aboard, thrusting cards at us, generally beseeching us to use this chandlery and those laundry facilities. We were more interested in receiving practique and getting ashore to collect mail at the post office.

Although the island is picturesque, we were not impressed with the people, nor our experiences. There were more extremes of wealth and poverty than we were accustomed to. Beggars swarmed the market area and I was frequently asked for money while I was shopping. Down-town Port Louis was dirty, with peeling paint, litter on the streets, rats and cockroaches, the shops dusty and congested. When we enquired of a harbour official, where should we place our garbage, he pointed to the harbour water.

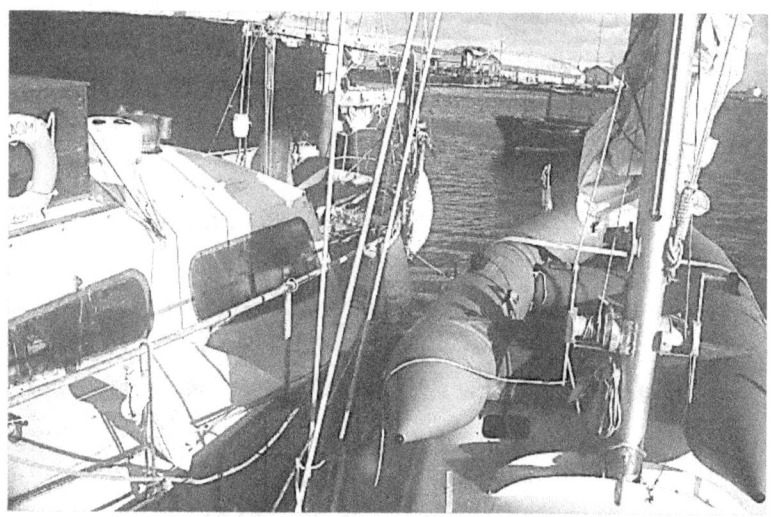

Caprice moored alongside Naomi, Port Louis

ne Sunday night, we decided to go to a restaurant with Mogens and Marianne, our neighbours on the American yacht, *Naomi*, leaving their family and crew as watch over both vessels.

Firstly, the taxi driver took us to the restaurant. Only on arrival did he inform us that it was closed. Then he charged us again to drive us back to a restaurant within walking distance of the harbour. There, we found the service to be fairly good, but both the food and the wine left a lot to be desired. We didn't enjoy the evening very much.

In order to do some sight-seeing, we decided to hire a motor-cycle. Although we'd made arrangements for the hiring and the time we'd collect the bike, it was not ready. After one hour of waiting while minor repairs were made, then papers filled out, we managed to leave. We drove only five miles before the rear tyre went flat.

Fortunately, Ian had carried his own tools and puncture repair kit with him, for there was nothing on the bike. When he had removed the worn tyre, he found a mass of patches on the tube. Glass and a tack were embedded in the tyre. The puncture repaired, we returned to the hire shop, irate at the condition of the tyre and tube. Eventually, the owner of the shop became apologetic and loaned us another bike, so we did manage to view some of the island.

The next episode which thoroughly disillusioned us was when both yachts arranged to get water from a warehouse close to where we were tied up. Our draught was too deep for us to lie alongside the harbour tap, yet the water launch supplied only big ships. Rather than ferry water in the dinghy, we made an arrangement with the warehouse caretaker.

When the tanks were full, he demanded 50 rupees (approx. A$15) which we are sure went straight into his pocket.

Korean fishing boats in Port Louis, Mauritius

After ten days in that filthy harbour, assaulted day and night with loud Korean music from the fishing fleet, we thankfully dropped our mooring and set off to sea again, scrubbing off the oily mess and throwing garbage overboard when we were clear of the harbour. Thereafter, we referred to the place as *Port Lousy*.

Although Reunion is reputed to be very beautiful, we were not prepared for further excursions on land among non-English speaking people so soon after our experiences in Mauritius, so we altered course to sail south of that island. Conditions were brisk with occasional squalls. For several hours, *Caprice* roared along on a broad reach at seven to eight knots. Naturally, the steering system could not cope with that, but once we were clear of Reunion and able to alter course for the South African coast, we were able to relax again.

We had been underway for three days when the wind fell off, and only by working hard for it, did we make any progress. I took sextant sights and painstakingly worked them; it was the first time I'd tried the complete navigation exercise. The result of my calculations put our position on the high veldt in South Africa. Several days of variable winds and calms followed. During the latter, we slept a lot, for Ian in particular was still weak from flu contracted in Mauritius.

Our first gale in the Indian Ocean found us about one hundred sea miles south of the island of Madagascar. Water poured through the ill-sealed fore hatch as we pitched and pounded into a westerly wind and sea. I was quite seasick for the first time since leaving Western Australia. When the wind began to scream in the rigging at 3.00 a.m. and the occasional wave was washing the decks, we decided to heave to. Ian recorded in the log that under storm jib and double-reefed main, *Caprice* was making five knots, so he put up the trysail, but we were tired enough after a few hours not to try sailing in such rough conditions and remained hove to all the next day.

We kept the trysail up to steady our motion and although we observed that our trolled fishing line was streaming out from abeam instead of astern, we didn't consider that our rate of sideways drift could be more than one knot. We had been nearly a hundred sea miles from the shipping path when we hove to, so watch-keeping for ships was rather lax. We nearly jumped out of our skins when a ship's siren sounded very close by. Racing out into the cockpit, we saw a black hull with the registration port of *Tonsberg*, but the freighter disappeared so quickly in the swells, we didn't have time to read her name. She altered course after she passed, so presumably had come to have a look at us. Normally, we assume that no ships will see us, and so take total responsibility for keeping ourselves out of their way.

A two metre swell would probably be quite sufficient to mask us from any ship's watch-keeping. At that stage we didn't have a radar reflector, not having been able to find one we considered adequate. In South Africa, Ian found time to design and make one, which could be dismantled to stow flat. We remained hove to again the next day, mainly out of laziness, for the wind and seas were abating. After our scare with the Norwegian ship, we kept a more regular watch, as we realized we must have drifted north into the shipping channel which passes south of the Malagasy Republic (formerly Madagascar.

After fifty five hours of being hove to, we got under way again. By noon, we were able to see the horizon for long enough to take a sight. To our astonishment, we found our position to be east of Port Dauphin, Malagasy Republic and by late afternoon, land was in sight to the west. As the wind moved further south, we were better able to lay a course to clear the southern end of the large island. Having planned to pass a hundred sea miles to the south of the land, we were rather disgusted with ourselves that night to see the lights of Port Dauphin and its fishing fleet.

The night was spectacular. Occasionally large black clouds masked the brilliant moon, then its white light shone on the black sea, lighting up the lace curtains of spray being flung aside by the bow as we plunged south west.

We had obviously experienced considerable current as well as leeward drift during the time we were hove to, so Ian decided to brush up on his star navigation in order to augment the sun sights as we neared the African coast. Mogens of *Naomi* had reminded him of the simple expedient of turning the sextant upside down during a star sight so that one brings the horizon up to the star, thus enabling one to keep the star within view. However, we didn't have volume one of the 249 Sight Reduction Tables, so the working of star sights had to be completed by the long admiralty method.

By the time we cleared the southern tip of Malagasy, we'd been at sea for twelve days. Although we were helped by a very strong current the next day (75 sea miles more than we logged), it took us a further nine days to reach Durban. Between squalls, there were frequent periods of calm or very light winds. With having to spend so much time at the tiller and changing sail, we were tired.

One night, although Ian warned me he was about to tack, I was so sleepy I didn't put up my canvas lee cloth. When *Caprice* heeled to the opposite tack, I fell out of bed, deeply bruising my shoulder and wrist.

Frequently, we didn't change sails when squalls approached, since they usually lasted only ten or fifteen minutes. In the variable conditions, we found we needed to make the most of those squalls in order to maintain reasonable progress. Of course, the inevitable happened. What Ian originally judged to be a temporary squall was something more. I awoke just before dawn to the roaring of water and wind. *Caprice* was well heeled, making at least six knots. I was just about to call Ian to see if he needed any assistance in changing sails, when there was a loud bang.

Oh my God, the mast's gone! I thought, then as Ian swung *Caprice* around, heaving her to, I knew for sure it was some kind of rigging failure. Thank heavens it was not the mast but the port backstay, which parted where a small piece of wire and hook had been swaged on. The hook had been used by the previous owner to support the boom, taking the place of a topping lift or boom gallows.

When daylight came, we found the badly frayed upper end of the stay (1X19 stainless) had tied itself around the topping lift, the starboard backstay and the radio aerial insulator. Quite a mess! Conditions were not ideal for climbing the mast. With the wind at twenty knots, moderate seas and no steadying sail, the motion was quite severe. Nevertheless, Ian rigged the boatswain's chair to a three purchase block and tackle, and then pulled himself up. It took him an hour to free the backstay and secure it with a bulldog-clip to another piece of rigging wire. By the time he was back on deck, Ian was exhausted and severely bruised. Several times, the motion had caused him to lose his grip on the mast, flinging the boatswain's chair out like a pendulum until it crashed against the mast again. The wooden seat had pinched his thighs against the mast, bruising them and causing bleeding.

As we neared the African coast, the western horizon took on a strange hue. The barometer was dropping, so we assumed bad weather was on its way. An ominous sunset showed yellow, orange, then blood red. Next morning, there was a thick haze in all directions, but no sign of land. Ian, being an Australian, ought to have recognised those signs as smoke haze. We were becoming rather concerned about our position after a brisk day's sailing and no horizon for sextant sights. Our Radio Direction Finder and our last known position concurred on the angle for Durban, but the Agulhas current is notorious, so we had laid a course for Cape St. Lucia lighthouse, about 80 sea miles to the north. After our experience with currents on the N.S.W. coast, we were prepared to be whisked south at any time. Imagine our relief when we sighted the light just after dark. At sunset, we were just five miles off the coast, yet still we were unable to see the land.

Not long after we had turned south, the wind dropped off preliminary to the approach of a cold front the next evening. Five hours of gale force winds arrived from just east of south.

At dawn of our twenty second day out of Mauritius, we were within sight of the city of Durban. With the wind on the nose, we gave up attempts to tack through the roads and motored into the harbour where we were met by the harbour police launch and shown to a mooring where we should await customs and immigration officials.

The initial entry requirements fulfilled, we were directed to the Point Yacht Club, which offers its facilities to visitors from all over the world. We and a number of other yachties on world circumnavigations were to make use of the hospitality for many months through 1975.

World-wide inflation forced us all to seek work. The very low cost of living in South Africa made it an ideal place to save money and we saved enough to complete our voyage.

Ian and I both accepted professional employment with the Durban City Council. With seventeen land-based months ahead of us and the knowledge that crossing oceans was not as hair-raising as sailing the N.S.W. coast, we decided to have our first child before leaving South Africa. Miraculously, everything went according to plan.

Caprice rafted outside larger yachts in Durban

We took Caprice out of the water so she could be overhauled, while we lived in a small flat close to the yacht club. I worked for a full twelve months before Jamie's birth in November 1975, while Ian continued until the end of December.

January 1976 was spent preparing for the notorious Durban to Cape Town run with its threat of strong currents, gales, freak waves and fogs. Many were the stories of huge freighters being broken up in that area, not to mention yachts bent, broken, abandoned or sunk.

The Suez Canal had not then re-opened, so all commercial shipping was still using the southerly route. This meant that watch-keeping on a small yacht entailed great vigilance. I was very reluctant to sail to Cape Town with a tiny baby, so we found two enthusiastic teenagers to accompany Ian while I drove overland in our battered old Kombi van.

Although yachts arriving in Cape Town both before and after *Caprice* suffered from bad conditions and damage (one pitch-poled, another grazed the side of a freighter), Ian had an unexpectedly pleasant trip in light to moderate conditions. His big triumph, I think, was to sail round the Cape of Good Hope under spinnaker!

Nine days after leaving Durban, Ian tied *Caprice* up in the yacht basin of the Royal Cape Yacht Club. That day, force ten winds were sweeping down from Table Mountain and across the bay, a localized phenomenon with which we became quite familiar during our four week stay in Cape Town.

We were guests aboard this tugboat in Cape Town.

Jan and Ian on deck, Durban

7 The South Atlantic

We wave goodbye with oil blackened hands. We have just let go our mooring lines from our marina berth at The Royal Cape Yacht Club. Someone is ringing the club bell. Clang! Clang! Clang! I see Ruth waving from the steps. Carol is back on *Landfall*. Colin, Wayne and Bill wave from the jetty. Chris and Graeme stand in the cockpit of *Clear Skies*. Everyone is wishing us a good trip; envious of our going; thankful they are still in port with lots of fresh water, milk, bread and meat; wishing they were away from the soot and the dust and the wind off Table Mountain. It is February 18, 4pm, before we motor out of the harbour, two years and two weeks after leaving Sydney. The baby kills our preference for early morning departures. We have the sails up, but there isn't enough wind to push us clear of the ships. One leaves just behind us, another enters. A fat, rusty, old lady lies at anchor just outside. Our engine is working well. Soon we are clear of the breakwaters and Robben Island with its dreaded prison lies ahead. I get out the camera and take a picture of the port lying beneath Table Mountain.

Jamie lies in his cot under the chart table, looking very bewildered, comforted only when he can see one of us to reassure himself. What will it be like for him at sea? Will I cope? Will we have enough water? "Ian,' did you fill the jerry cans with water as well as the tank?"

"Did I fill the tank? I thought you had"'

"But when I saw you with the hose, I asked if you'd done the water. Didn't you say yes'?"

"I said no!"

Oh hell! And to think I had carefully avoided using the pump from that time on. Just as well we'd filled the tank only two days before. But I'd been using water with abandon. Too late to turn back now. Our clearance time was up at 5pm. Ian would have to repeat all those forms, all that walking from office to office all over Cape Town.

We measured the water.

It was 16cm from the top. *Twenty five litres, maybe more used. Thank goodness I picked up the five litres in the cracked plastic container,* intending to throw away the container when the water was used. We must stop at St. Helena now, rollers or no rollers. We'll have to wait until we can land. Anyway, Jamie has to have his next triple antigen injection.

Soon the sky clouded over. A bank of mist lay near the peninsular. I shivered, looked for pullovers and hoped we wouldn't get fog. It had been foggy until late morning and the foghorn at Green Point had been droning mournfully for hours. But the Assistant Port Captain had assured Ian that there would be no fog that night. We could leave. And he was right. However, the sky was overcast most of the night and it was very cold, even in two woollen pullovers, heavy waterproofs and woollen socks. We kept deck watch all night. Ian described the early part of the night as 'like King's Cross on a Friday night' because there were so many ships. It was hard to keep awake. For days, we had been so frantically busy getting ready. Now, I wanted to sleep. A ship seemed to be coming directly astern. I panicked, wanted the engine on because we had so little steerage in the light breeze, but it passed slowly to starboard at a safe distance.

The next day, we didn't see so many ships. Visibility was restricted and it rained. At least quite a lot of soot was washed away with the rain and there was wind. That night, there were still ships about, but the sky was clear, starlit and the moon rose at 10pm when I got up to take over watch from Ian. It was still quite cold and there were seals swimming nearby.

A large ship was passing across our bows – right in our path. Ian turned on the navigation lights and altered course. He wouldn't go below until we were clear. We weren't actually on a collision course, but too close for comfort. As the ship passed, they put a spotlight on us. It was good to know they were keeping watch and had seen us. Our radar reflector must be working.

By the second morning, we seemed to have passed across all the shipping lanes. All day, we saw no more ships, no more seals and no more land, just birds and endless ocean.

My diary entry on Saturday, February 21, 1976 reads: *Today, I feel tired again. Yesterday, I was so busy; I washed and dried all the nappies, cleaned the mooring lines of oil and started writing. All afternoon, I have felt fuzzy in the head. I suppose it is the change in motion. This morning, the wind turned to the S.E. Ian was singing when I awoke.*

'We've picked up the 'trades',' he joyfully exclaimed, 'the S.E. trades!'

We decided to have breakfast before setting the twin running jibs. Despite the increase in ocean temperature, the yoghurt I'd bought in Cape Town five days before was still fresh. But my locker against the hull under the galley was no longer chill. I had lost my refrigerator so soon. It is an ill wind … We were able to walk about barefoot without our feet becoming numb. It took a couple of hours to lay out the extra sheet ropes and rig the running poles. Ian had new poles made up in Durban, with proper topping lifts, downhauls and outhauls. Now he was able to rig the poles, then attach the sails and pull them out. So much safer than before, when he used to attach the sail to one end of the pole, then wave it in the air until he was able to snap the other end onto the mast ring.

Instead of sleeping that afternoon as I would have liked, I gave Jamie a sponge bath – his first in salt water. I had hoped it would be warm enough to put his bath in the cockpit, but the temperature hadn't risen above 23 degrees and after a daily 35 degrees in Cape Town, it seemed rather chilly, especially with a cool wind astern.

Jamie seemed to be settling down to the motion after five days at sea. He was not nearly as fractious as I'd anticipated, and had already returned to his smiling, cheerful, gurgling self. As for Ian and me – tired, oh so tired! We wanted to sleep all the time.

I suppose it was nervous reaction to the previous four or five months which were so hectic. The rolling motion under the running sails made us both slightly queasy and Ian became depressed after his initial elation as we wondered listlessly if all the discomfort were worth it. To me, that night, even suburbia began to seem desirable...well, not quite.

Although we were averaging 100 sea miles per day, our sun sights showed us to be close to the shipping lanes again. Ian assumed that we were experiencing some sideways drift, as well as the northerly current, but we had no real idea how much since our *Sumlog* cable snapped the first day out of Cape Town. (Later, our ability to estimate the dead reckoning without a log became quite accurate.)

When I came up at 11pm to take over watch from Ian, there was a ship on the starboard quarter which appeared to be moving slowly on a parallel course. The masthead lights were well separated and the port lights visible. We decided that she should pass sufficiently clear of us, so Ian went below. Just before he was ready to go to sleep, I told Ian that the ship was nearly abeam and about a mile off. However, instead of moving further ahead, she seemed to come sideways very rapidly.

By the time I'd woken Ian again, to switch on our navigation lights, the ship was alongside with a spotlight on us. Until that light went on, I imagined that I had misinterpreted their lights, and that it was a case of converging courses. I was quite shaken because there was very little evasive action we could take without dropping the running sails and putting on the engine. One just can't tack with twin jibs out on poles!

Thank goodness Ian's addition of an auxiliary rudder to the standard QME steering system was working well. We had to do much less hand steering. With it working so well, even in light conditions, the sailing of the boat seemed to have taken itself over.

"*Caprice* is now independent," I recorded in my journal. "We are merely along for the ride."

Our heads had been far too fuzzy to worry about trolling a fishing line while we were in the cold Benguela current, where marine life abounded. Once into the trade wind zone, birds were much rarer, so we assumed that fish would be too.

We began to see flying fish, although at first they were far too tiny for cooking. Later, I used to cook the sardine-sized ones for Jamie. The toe-rail on *Caprice* is too low to retain any bigger ones that might have landed on deck during the night.

The fresh bread we bought in Cape Town lasted 12 days! It is quite the best value for money in food that we've seen, being a heavy whole crushed wheat loaf costing only 11c. The South African Government subsidises it for the non-whites, but the ironic part is that the non-whites prefer to eat refined white bread and it is the whites who tend to buy the brown bread.

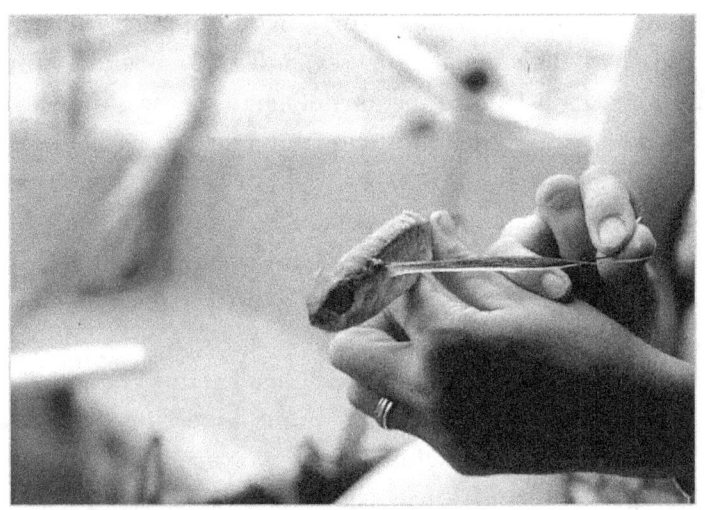

Jan holds a flying fish

We'd been at sea for 10 days when the wind fell quite light, and remained so until we reached St. Helena. It was as I'd imagined the trade wind belt of the South Atlantic: long swells, a clear blue sky with just a scattering of cloud and a relentlessly hot sun. By 9am, I was becoming sunburned, so we pulled out the cockpit awning I'd made in Durban. How sweet the shade, but the awning reeked of Cape Town's soot, bringing back memories of steam-train journeys during my childhood in New Zealand.

We sail under a spinnaker, set with twin poles

Seventeen days out of Cape Town, we sighted St. Helena. We'd been sailing with the spinnaker for seven days! The wind followed us as we rounded the island to the anchorage in the north-west, so that we lowered the spinnaker only to motor into the harbour. What a fantastic run that had been; 1700 sea miles in 17 days. As we came in, we recognised a small French yacht, *Kantread,* which had been in Durban, Cape Town and St Helena. A local boat came out to lead us to a mooring and soon we were catching up on the news of other yachting acquaintances.

Napoleon's place of exile is usually made out to be rather bleak. We found the island to be quite charming especially the site of his residence, which we visited with another two yachties. The people too, were friendly and courteous. They were able to provide most provisions that we required, so long as we gave them sufficient advance notice.

The landing place was not difficult and when we mentioned the pilot book's reference to rollers, the locals assured us that they had never seen any more than a few feet high.

I could not help comparing St. Helena with Rodrigues. In St. Helena, we found no hankering for the fast pace of life and commercialism. They had electricity, a part-time radio broadcast station, telephone, movies three times a week, a hospital, cars and motorcycles, and a mail and passenger ship twice per month. Cargo and fishing boats call occasionally. There is also the advantage that whilst the island is high enough to draw rain from the trade winds, it does not get hurricanes.

Jamie received his injection and polio vaccine, making him very fractious when we were trying to prepare to leave after our five-day visit. We would have preferred to wait another night before leaving, except for the yachtie superstition against leaving port on a Friday. Consequently, by the time we raised sail at 5pm on Thursday evening, our tempers were sorely frayed.

Jamestown, St Helena

Jamie meets a Galapagos Tortoise in St Helena

From St. Helena to Ascension Island, we made a brisk passage under the twin jibs, *Caprice* once again performing like a roller-coaster on a corkscrew. The weather became very humid so that for the first time I was unable to get Jamie's nappies dry.

Our first sight of Ascension was of the lights at the US satellite tracking station. Mistaking them for a fishing vessel, we altered course to the east, consequently having to sail back when we sighted land the next morning. It was close to midday when we tied up in the 'anchorage'. There is no holding ground there at all and we were told of yachts drifting seawards, dragging their anchors. Two yachts were on moorings when we arrived: *Kantread*, which left for the Azores within an hour of our arrival, and *Rama Zulu*, built and sailed by a lone South African woman, Anna Woolf.

Ian went ashore alone to see the officials, then the next morning, Anna helped us ashore with Jamie. Clinging onto a dangling rope, one had to leap onto steep narrow steps at the top of the two-metre swell. We were very glad to have a rubber dinghy. All our purchases had to be thrown into the dinghy before we jumped off the step. Ian jumped first, then, my heart in my mouth, I threw the baby to him. Next I jumped and we pushed the dinghy clear of the rocks.

That night, we experienced some bigger 'rollers'. It was windy with rain, and the swells grew to about four or five metres. Ian spent several hours trying to prevent Anna's boat being damaged by a barge. She was unable to help, being trapped ashore at the time. All the next day, it was impossible to get ashore.

We were not impressed with Ascension, which is British-owned, but home for an American base. The British, the Americans and the St. Helenian work-force each have their separate social groups, none of which appeared interested in the yachts. The landscape is almost lunar, with bare brown hills of lava on which nothing grows.

The next morning at dawn, we were hailed and arose to find *Landfall* looking for a mooring. After keeping Carol, Wayne and baby company for another day, we were happy to set sail again and be free of that rolling anchorage.

This time, our destination was Barbados, the eastern most island of the West Indies. We covered the distance of just over 3000 sea miles in record time – 27 days. It was a relatively uneventful passage, during which I in particular, fell prone to the sense of timelessness, which we've found prevails during tropical sailing. Relatively simple events during this time are written up in my journal as though of significance; e.g. the successful cooking of pancakes.

Evenings I found exhilarating. Once Jamie was asleep for the night, we would relax over coffee and liqueur in the starlight. It was so warm and humid that we required no more than underclothes, even at night. Often, I would stand in the cockpit, the wind gently buffeting my body as I watched the silver crested waves in the moonlight. There is something hypnotic about it, even when the occasional wave is lopped into the cockpit, so that one stands and watches for yet the next wave and inevitably, gets showered.

We worried unnecessarily about the time it would take for us to pass through the doldrums' zone between the S.E. and the N.E. trades. On April 2, when I went off watch at dawn, the wind was from the S.E. When I awoke to get breakfast two hours later, it was from the N.E. What incredible luck! The following day, we had a double celebration: it was Ian's 29th birthday and we crossed the equator that morning. In our usual fashion at sea, we celebrated by eating and drinking special goodies. This time, to mellow the occasion, we had duty-free Glen Fiddich, bought in Ascension for two guineas (£2.20) a bottle. Also, about a week before, I tried cooking a rum and raisin cake in the frying pan. (We have no oven.) It certainly didn't have much time to mature, but tasted good nevertheless.

This section of the voyage was our only period of successful fishing. For the first time, we organised a trip-line so that when a fish took the lure, we heard the line snap out to its full length. The fish in the area were so plentiful that I could plan to have fish for dinner before we trolled the line. On several occasions, we got a bite even before the line was properly set up.

Our first catch was a dorado about 1.25 metres long and weighing 10 kilos. Unfortunately, we are both very inexperienced at fishing, so that the gaffing, killing and cutting up of the fish resulted in a lot of mess. Nor did we, at that stage, know how to go about drying the flesh.

We ate double portions for four consecutive meals, then reluctantly threw the remainder overboard. It was more than a week before we felt like trolling the line again. Altogether, we caught several dorado (often called dolphin fish), a bonito and a barracuda.

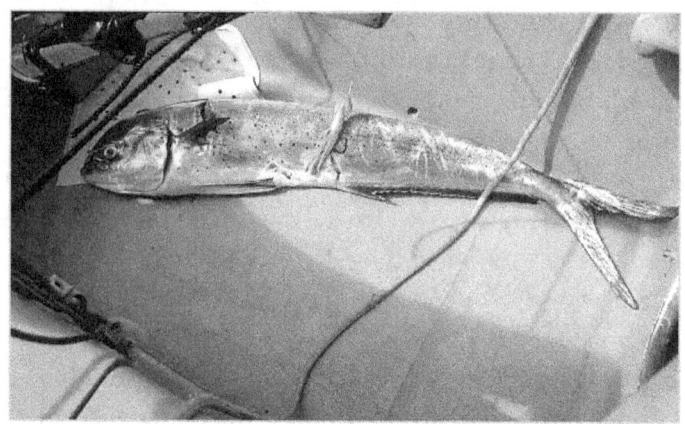
Dorado or dolphin fish

As we approached Barbados, we encountered a new navigational difficulty. With the sun directly overhead, it was almost impossible to get a noon sight. The azimuth changed approximately 160 degrees in the ten minutes around noon. We were forced to rely on star sights, but on several occasions, there was too much cloud. The weather became quite changeable and our daily mileage dropped.

One evening while I was on watch, I listened to the BBC. An announcement made me realize that it was Easter. How strange that we'd been out of contact with other people for so long, we didn't know.

Bridgetown Harbour, Barbados

On Easter Monday we dropped anchor at Bridgetown, expecting to wait until the next day for clearance, but the officials came out to us that morning. That there was no fee even on a holiday was a pleasant surprise.

8 The West Indies: The Windward Antilles

Barbados disappeared behind us in a haze. Our course was set for Carriacou in the Grenadines. Despite our premonitions that we wouldn't like Barbados, we had found it a most pleasant island and stayed ten days.

Paul of *Albatross* was there. We also came to know Dave and Mavis of *Pom*, who were sailing a cat home to Sydney from England, and Lindy and Michael Couch of *Pascarus*, from England. The latter proved to be a really friendly couple.

Customs came and cleared us on the Tuesday morning after our arrival. Later, Paul introduced us to Terry and Alan, who ran an unofficial club for cruising yachties. They were marine and diesel engineers with a place right near the small craft fuel jetty.

The pair made yachties welcome and we were able to use their fridge and shower. The sitting room was comfortably battered, decorated with flags, post cards and many other mementos from visiting yachts. There was also a dart board.

Prices of foodstuffs (even local produce) and most other things we found it necessary to buy in Bridgetown were about double that in South Africa. Yet, we were assured that canned goods were even dearer in the other islands. Mostly, we stocked up on flour, sugar and rice. The rum was beautiful though – about $2 per bottle for quality we've never even seen in Australia. We bought 1 1/4 gallons in the hope that it would last until we reached the U.S.A. It didn't.

The anchorage was clean with good holding, the water so clear, it was very inviting. The new moon caused an increase in swell, but mostly we and our boat were rocked by the wash from water skiers and fishing boats.

On Thursday, I visited the baby clinic, where Jamie received his final dose of triple antigen and the oral polio vaccine. He was off colour and quite miserable for two or three days after. When he was over his reaction to the injection, we decided to do some sightseeing.

Local bus was the only transport possibility. Taxis and hire cars were both prohibitively expensive, being geared to the American and continental tourists' pockets. None of the bus routes were interlinking. Each goes out from Bridgetown, then returns by the same route. We managed to fit in two journeys. In the morning, we went to Sam Lord's castle on the south east coast. Sam Lord was an opportunist who, to lure sailing ships onto the reef early in the 19th century, set up lights in imitation of those for Carlisle Bay. He then sent out his slaves to slaughter the crews and plunder the wrecks.

With some of his accumulated wealth, Lord built a very large house on the headland. This has now been turned into an expensive tourist hotel and park. The ground floor of the hotel was set up as museum. We were charged B$2.00 each to enter the grounds. Later, we went down to the beach where there is a snack bar, with the intention of buying a sandwich for lunch. However, sandwiches cost B$2.50 each and a coke, which is 25c in town, cost 75c. I felt decidedly irked by the place, considering it a huge swindle even by normal tourist standards. They are certainly continuing Sam Lord's tradition.

In the afternoon, we took another bus right across the island to Bathsheba, a village on the east coast. The driver of the second bus (another company) was even more reckless than the first. School was just out and it was raining, so there were a lot of children on board. I have never seen a bus packed like that one. It had open sides (canvas rolled down to protect the passengers in wet weather) and the seats were benches extending right across the vehicle, normally seating eight people each. At one stage, there must have been nearly a hundred people in and clinging onto that bus! We rode through sugar cane country and mountains – quite different to the coastal area, where we saw cotton growing for seed.

After departing Barbados, we sailed all night and in the morning we caught sight of Sail Rock through the mist. It was a very fortunate sighting which verified our position, for most of the land was still shrouded in mist.

We passed through the Martinique channel and dropped anchor in Hillsborough Bay on the northern side of Carriacou. In the channel, we saw, for the first time, the big local trading schooners. What a picture they made under full sail on blue waters amid coconut palm-fringed green islands! Carriacou is the northern-most island of the group and is governed by Grenada. When Ian went ashore to complete entrance formalities, he was advised that Tyrell Bay was a better anchorage. We decided to go there the following day and subsequently arrived in that harbour about midday.

Trading Schooners in Tyrell Bay, Carriacou (Grenada)

Although it was May Day, the locals held a beachside market when the trading schooner arrived from Grenada at 2.00pm. We went ashore, bought fresh fruit and vegetables, and then proceeded to walk as far as we were able in the heat with the burden of Jamie in the pack on Ian's back. The women and children seemed to be fascinated at seeing Jamie in the backpack. I even heard one group of small children arguing as to whether he was a baby or a doll!

On Saturday evening, a teenage boy called to us to ask if we wished to buy conch. We invited him on board and he chatted for half an hour or so. It transpired that his father owned the big local trading sloop anchored in the bay, and the boy was most interested in navigation using sextant and compass, since his father used neither. That aroused our interest, so we arranged to visit his father's boat the following morning.

On Sunday morning, we duly arose early to get the routine chore of nappy washing done before rowing across to *Baby Light* where Johnny, his father and brother awaited us. They found Ian's interest difficult to understand – also his accent, so I tried to explain that there are few places in the world today where such boats as theirs are built for commercial purposes – certainly not in Australia where few people, if any, know how to use the adze. Since they had not yet breakfasted, we invited them back for coffee on *Caprice*. Johnny's father had never been below on a cruising yacht before, although he certainly seemed very familiar with the deck layout and fittings.

The West Indies Working Schooner, Baby Light

It was close to 12.30 before we pulled in the anchor and set sail for Hillsborough again, where we had to get our clearance. At 3.30, we raised the anchor for the second time that afternoon and headed across the Martinique channel to Union island. It was a hard beat against wind, sea and current, so eventually, we resorted to using the motor. To say that the hour between 5.30 and 6.30 was rather tense is an understatement. The sun set at 6.12pm and we had to enter a channel 150m wide between low-lying coral reef to get into Clifton Harbour. In the rapidly fading light, Ian almost missed seeing the buoy which, typically, was not lit when it should have been. I stood on the bow to guide us in, and night was upon us by the time the anchor was down. Our neighbour, the owner of a 15m charter boat, came over to welcome us and told us a little of his chartering experience.

The next day, we also met his friend who was employed to skipper another 15m charter vessel. The lines of a third large yacht appealed to us – a beautifully constructed steel ketch. We begged an introduction and spent an interesting evening on board. The interior layout was of course geared to chartering, so I learned nothing there and it was too dark and wet for Ian to see much of the deck. However, another French couple with a small daughter was also present and on Tuesday morning we took a look at their boat.

She was also steel. Hugo had adapted a Quarto design and had the hull built in Lyons. The interior design was one of the most interesting I've seen for a 9m boat. Of course Hugo had designed the layout specifically for cruising. Features we found worthy of note were the workbench which converts to a chart table (not vice versa); a system of double drawers, one sliding in behind the other; and the way the stove was gimballed over a 'U' shape. Both hatches were domed for ease of looking out in bad weather.

Apart from the town itself, we saw very little of Union Island. We set off in the early afternoon for Mustique, but soon realised that it would be too difficult to beat across there, so we settled for a tiny bay just north of the main anchorage, Canouan. I took the tiller while Ian stood on the bow ready to drop the anchor. He kept motioning me closer and closer to the shore until suddenly there was a soft thud and he was furiously telling me to reverse. I cut the engine, but of course had to wait for the rotation to stop before I could start her in reverse. (This is a peculiarity of the Dolphin engine.) We were aground! I opened the throttle, but we didn't move. More throttle, then slowly we backed off. Ian reacted by waiting until we were three quarters out of the bay before dropping the anchor.

Fed up, I decided to swim ashore and go for a walk. I tied my thongs around my waist and dived in. It was much further than it appeared and I was tiring as I neared the shore. I was about to feel for the bottom when I looked down through the clear water. I had almost stepped onto a bed of sea urchins. There was no way across them. With renewed vigour, I swam back to *Caprice*. My desire to go ashore had waned somewhat. Ian dived to check the keel for damage, but could find only a small scratch. She appeared to be quite okay.

We moved on to Admiralty Bay, Bequia, the next day, where we anchored mid-afternoon. Later that evening, another small yacht entered the bay, carrying the Dutch flag. They had also come up from Canouan, where we'd noticed them sail into the next bay the previous afternoon. They had two children on a 7.5m sloop, so we soon got talking and visited them the next afternoon. Their boat certainly made far less use of the available space than *Caprice*. They had bought the boat in Arula, Netherlands Antilles, to cruise the Leeward Islands, then sell her before returning to Holland. On Friday morning, they returned the visit and had coffee with us.

Local boat careened. Notice the ballast stones on the shore

Admiralty Bay, although quite crowded with yachts, was an anchorage with a lot of charm. We were very interested to see a local trading boat careened on the beach, its ballast stones in a pile beside it. These stones are carefully saved and used again and again, for there are no suitable stones available in the islands. The stones originally came from Europe in the sailing ships.

In the evening, local musicians visited the charter yachts, so for the first time, we were regaled with Caribbean music.

Our next stop was St. Lucia. I didn't like the idea of leaving on a Friday and began to feel seasick even before we had the anchor up. It was blowing briskly. We tried to sail away from the anchorage, but after coming close to putting ourselves aground, we motored out. It turned into a rough, wet and thoroughly uncomfortable night of beating. We decided to go to leeward of St Vincent rather than risk onshore winds and currents on an unlit coast. Poor little Jamie was not the least bit happy about sailing in such conditions and nor was I.

In the morning, when land eventually appeared, we realised that it would take all day to beat against the current to Vieux Port where we'd intended to enter St. Lucia, so we continued up the coast. Once in the lee of the island, the seas calmed completely, then the wind dropped, so we motored the rest of the way into Marigot Bay, a delightful haven almost invisible from the sea. A narrow channel opens up into one of the loveliest secluded anchorages I have seen. Last century, the British navy used it as a hideout.

We stayed at Marigot for the weekend, but didn't leave the boat except to swim. To begin with, teenage boys pestered us to buy fresh produce at very inflated prices (they didn't know of a figure less than $2.00), but when they realised I was not going to pay more than market prices, they left us alone. As Marigot is not a port of entry, we were worried that a coastal patrol launch might find us there, so we pulled out early on Monday morning.

Somehow, we misinterpreted the landmarks and sailed past the entrance to Castries, the capital of St. Lucia. We spent several hours close hauled to get back again. When we arrived, no one questioned Ian's statement that we'd left Bequia on Sunday.

Ian was almost talked into paying E.C. $15.00 for a tiny St. Lucia courtesy flag. Each little nation, expects visiting yachts to fly their flag at the crosstrees, so I was kept busy making them from scraps of spinnaker sail material I carried for that purpose.

The water at Castries was murky, but I leapt over the side for a swim and hair wash. Ian swam too and then we gave Jamie a dip. Later, a fellow came by to tell us that the water was not safe for swimming because of the sewerage in the bay. However, none of us had any ill effects.

9 The Leeward Antilles

After a day of shopping and visiting other cruising yachts, we had an early night and got under way from Castries straight after breakfast. The passage to Martinique was good – no beating but fairly close hauled. HMS Diamond Rock is a mighty landmark. There was no mistaking our position.

HMS Diamond Rock

We rounded Cape Solomon in the early afternoon, then seeing a bay and town, assumed this was Fort de France, capital of the French West Indies. Ian laid out the anchor and we put up the flags. Next thing, a police launch approached us and we soon got the message that Fort de France was the next bay north. We must go there first to enter. When we saw Fort de France, we realised that our mistake must have looked very stupid. The bay was huge — several kilometres across, and the city larger than Castries. By the time we were safely anchored it was too late to go ashore. Ian went next morning, armed with his French dictionary, to get clearance. He returned about an hour later, bringing a long crusty loaf of French bread, cheese and wine. Unable to resist, we sat down to sample it. We'd had breakfast but a very early lunch tasted so good!

In the afternoon, we all went ashore. Most people spoke no English at all, so it was very strange having to force myself into

French. I managed to ask at a bank for directions to a branch of Barclays where I changed some traveller's cheques. We went back to the small grocery shop and bought more bread, cheese, wine, ground coffee and yoghurt, then went to the market which was opposite for fresh fruit and vegetables. Next, we found a marine store where we purchased some *Terylene* line for sail gaskets. I thought the town picturesque and clean with its narrow streets and small shops. We were tired when we arrived back from shopping, but I made a salad and after Jamie went to bed, we sat in candlelight to eat bread, cheese, salami and salad. We drank wine and felt happy.

Next day, we shared a rum punch with another cruising couple, then back to *Caprice* for an early lunch. We sailed off our anchorage with no mishaps, so I think we are improving our skills a little.

I am not keen on overnight sailing in these waters, so I was pleased when, in the late afternoon, Ian decided to anchor at Rades de St. Pierre. It is a fairly open anchorage with swells on the beam, which wasn't at all comfortable. Without going ashore, we left Sunday morning straight after breakfast and had a slow, gentle passage across to Dominica. We had been warned that Dominica is very poor and the children insistent beggars, especially at Rupert Bay. I don't know how such a barren island can survive as an independent nation.

We dropped anchor at Roseau Roads, which was also a fairly open anchorage with beam swells. Most of the evening, we were assailed by the maniacal screaming of an over- amplified hell fire and damnation evangelical preacher. We were not tempted to go ashore.

From Roseau to Isles de Saintes is close to 65km, so we departed very early in the morning. It is unnerving to be able to see the bottom. The channel was well buoyed with lobster pot markers — right down the middle. Here was the main French fort and holing up place during the Napoleonic wars. I declined to climb the hill to Fort Napoleon with Ian.

Our next port was the British equivalent: Nelson's Dockyard in English Harbour, Antigua. We sailed all night guided by the lights of Guadeloupe, and Antigua was just visible the next morning.

While crossing the channel that morning, a splash of bright yellow caught our attention halfway between the two islands. we saw a rather unusual sight. Three men were in a tiny local fishing boat, with an outboard strapped to the stern. In that tropical heat at 10.00am, the three oil-skinned fishermen were trying to recover their oar from a shark. One fellow was hammering the beast over the head with his machete while another was pulling on the oar.

Nelson's Dockyard, English Harbour

Jamie explores unfamiliar stuff in Antigua – grass

English Harbour was not difficult to find, although it has a narrow entrance and is well sheltered. Paul of *Albatross* was still there, so we shared a bottle of wine with him but he declined dinner. We stayed several days at English Harbour. I found it a strange place with its mixture of eras. The Nicholson family who run it have restored many of the buildings to their former state then put them to modern usage. There's a grocery shop, chandlery, restaurant, bar, boutique, laundry, showers etc., as well as a museum and ship repair facilities. The old fort on Barclay's point is still in disrepair.

We made an overnight passage to St. Bartholomew (St. Barts), the northern-most island of the French West Indies. Gustavia, the main town, lies 145kms from English Harbour. I found St. Barts a magical island. I enjoyed our stay there better than any of the rest of the Antilles. Tourism is not a big industry, so the people are quite friendly.

Although Antigua was pretty, I felt antipathy towards the place. It was a man's world at English Harbour and I do not share Ian's interest in naval history. Moreover, it was the most expensive place we had been to for fresh produce and groceries. I got the feeling that visitors were being charged far higher prices than local people. St. Bart's prices for fresh fruit and vegetables were very high too, but were not inflated for visiting yachtsmen. Virtually nothing is grown on the island itself, so all fresh produce has to be shipped in from Guadaloupe. I joined the locals at the wharf-side market when the ship was unloaded.

Historically, St. Barts was French. The French gave it to the Swedes on the condition that it should remain a free port in perpetuity. Later, the Swedes returned it to the French, but the duty free conditions remained. I believe there is no income tax either. The island's chief source of revenue is from smuggling liquor. Barbados rum is bought tax free then smuggled back into Barbados and into other islands too at just under the normal retail price. Consequently, in St. Barts, we were able to buy Barbados rum (the best in the world) at U.S. $1.25 per bottle!

The day after our arrival was my 30th birthday, which Jamie celebrated by cutting his fourth tooth. We had intended to eat at a restaurant that evening, but we were invited to a beach-side barbeque which was much more relaxing with Jamie along.

During our stay, we got to know Paul Johnson and his 13m gaff ketch *Venus,* which he sails with his wife Barbara and their two year old son, Magnus. In *Cruising World,* we had read about Paul's previous venture of buying an old church in the USA then using the timber to build an 8m yacht. The present *Venus* is solid, practical and cheaply built to Paul's own design. She sails extremely well as we found out. Ian begged a ride with them when they sailed over to St. Martin and back one day. Paul is a true yachtsman, born and bred to the game and is capable of making a living out of it without compromising himself too much. He seemed to regard Ian as a kind of protégé and taught him a lot.

The anchorage at Gustavia, St Barts

Paul's friend, Lou Lou, is part of the magic of the island. Born there of French parents, Lou Lou is quietly spoken and gentle. An admirer par excellence of Che Guevara, he wears the green beret with a white star over his long red 'corkscrew' curls and, in this improbable military outfit, runs a very modern yacht chandlery. He has named his own yacht *Che.*

On Sunday afternoon, Lou Lou took the Johnsons, us and a couple of other people for a tour around the island. It is very dry, yet pretty in its own way.

The next weekend was the first anniversary of the island's 'revolution'. The revolution occurred because the doctor who had been on the island for a period of duty was recalled and replaced. His replacement was not popular, so the locals invited the former doctor to return after they packed up the new doctor and put him on a plane out. Three gendarmes, returned with the doctor to reinstate him. This incensed the local population, so the gendarmes sent a message asking for help. The French tried to fly in troops, but the plane was prevented from landing because the locals covered the landing strip with their cars. The French declared this a state of revolution and the troops were sent in by ship. As they waded ashore from the landing craft, the locals shut their shops and businesses, pulling down the shutters and retired into their homes for a week. During this time, the troops wandered the island, becoming more and more bored until finally they were recalled. The previous doctor returned under the conditions offered by the people of St. Bart's and thus ended the 'revolution'.

To mark the anniversary, there was a fishing competition held on the Friday, then on Sunday, a yacht race. Eight boats entered the race. I went on *Venus* with Jamie and Lou Lou arranged for two of his friends to crew for Ian on *Caprice*.

We had never raced *Caprice*, so we were interested in her performance, heavily laden and weed-bound as she was. Ian was last over the start line and continued to trail the field until the last lap, where the yachts were hard on the wind. There, the Top Hat pointed better than most of the other yachts and made up enough distance to finish the race in sixth place.

That evening, friends on the New Zealand yacht, *Ben Gunn* arrived and the next morning, the Australian yacht *Faraway*, owned by Brian and Judy Harrison, also anchored. We had intended to leave for the United States that day, but old friends are more important than keeping to schedule.

After swopping some books and saying our farewells, it was late in the afternoon that we motored out of the harbour to the outer bay, where we cleaned up one of the anchors, got the dinghy packed up with our survival gear and generally readied ourselves for an early departure. We set course for Morehead City, North Carolina on the 8th of June, 1976, having spent nearly two months wending our way through the Lesser Antilles.

10 Off to the USA

I was sad at leaving St. Bartholomew. It was the one island in the Lesser Antilles where I'd felt particularly relaxed and unhassled. We sailed out through the Anegada Passage between the Virgin Islands and the northern most section of the Antilles chain, leaving St. Martin, Anguilla and Sombrero to leeward.

Moving briskly on a broad reach, *Caprice*'s motion was rather uncomfortable, but we soon adapted to being at sea again. At first, watch keeping was quite onerous until we were clear of the major shipping route from Europe to Panama. After that, it was plain sailing. For the most part, we had good winds on the beam or quarter and on one occasion, used the spinnaker. Our daily runs kept to an average of 100 nautical miles so that it was exactly twelve days later we made our landfall in the United States.

The biggest problem we faced during the passage was Jamie's first illness. He was eight months old and in the throes of teething, so at first, I assumed that to be the cause of his irritability. By the time it dawned on me that he was really sick, we were too far from land to seek medical help. I began to feel that I'd been foolish to encourage Ian to sell the old double sideband band transmitter in Antigua, even though I knew from experience that its power consumption flattened our batteries in an impractically short period of time. When Jamie erupted in spots, I was very relieved, for with the help of Dr. Spock and our Ship Captains' Medical Guide, I was able to diagnose his illness as Rubella. By the time his spots had faded, Jamie was almost well, once again wearing a cheerful grin.

Fishing was both unsuccessful and frustrating, for we were crossing the edge of the Sargasso Sea. Every time the fishing line tripped, I found we'd hooked a large piece of weed.

Wary of Cape Hatteras and its fearsome reputation, we decided to enter the United States at the nearest port of entry south of there. This is Morehead, City in North Carolina where nearby Cape Lookout is marked by a lighthouse. Guided by the light, we entered Lookout Bay on Saturday night. At first, all the lights tallied with those shown on the chart (a new one) and we were confidently sailing across the bay to where we planned to anchor.

Our first surprise was to find that the breakwater had been extended a few hundred metres and the light which had formerly marked its end was still in the old position. A rapid tack took us clear and we rounded the extension. When we were close to our proposed anchorage, an area charted at three fathoms, we suddenly found ourselves aground in mud. I went into a complete panic with the thud, thud, thud of the keel, coming back to my senses only when Ian gave me the order to lower the jib which was still flapping.

Ian was preparing to unlash the dinghy in order to sound around the boat with the lead line, when I tentatively asked, 'Could we could try the engine first?'

Ian decided to do so and to our surprise, we pulled back into deeper water quite easily. Using the lead line this time, Ian found an area deep enough to anchor, then we lit our stern lantern and retired to our bunks, exhausted. It was 4.00a.m. Next morning, we found that where we'd gone aground was a new spoil area for a nearby dredged channel.

We spent that Sunday resting and cleaning up in preparation for entering at Morehead City the following day. Monday morning dawned with a low leaden sky. Between heavy squalls, we readied *Caprice* to sail across the bay to the port channel, a distance of three nautical miles. By the time Ian had raised the storm jib and the triple-reefed main, another squall hit. Visibility was almost nil at times. Ian was virtually blinded with the rain on his glasses, but I could occasionally pick out shoals and light structures sufficiently to recognise that current and leeward drift shoreward were considerable. I was almost sick with fear during that half hour. We had to point 25 degrees further into the wind to keep on course. Incredibly in that sharp, short sea, we found the lead buoys and with much relief; turned down the marked channel, the wind astern.

In the harbour, we anchored in the turning circle, our flags fluttering, to await the customs or Coast Guard. Soon, a Coast Guard vessel approached and towed away another yacht. It returned thirty minutes later, and approached us. Did we have something wrong with our engine? Pointing to our flags, Ian explained that we required customs and immigration. To our amazement, we realised that the Coast Guard officer had no idea what our yellow Q flag meant. I think he'd never before seen the Australian ensign.

There ensued a lengthy radio-telephone conversation via the shore station to customs, in which he described in detail our flags. Soon we were invited to follow the launch to Morehead City marina. There, we were met by a most pleasant Customs Official who firstly helped us tie up, then made very short work of the official papers. We were able to collect our six month cruising permit later that afternoon from his office across the street. We were most grateful when he waived any duty on the two cases of rum we'd brought from St. Bart's.

The next day, we went shopping. Morehead City is, despite its name, a fairly small town, but we found it quite big enough to initiate us into the consumer society of the U.S.A. Our first discovery was the distance we had to walk between shops. We were the only ones walking. The look right then left habit for crossing the road was so deeply ingrained, that several times I almost stepped in front of oncoming traffic. In the supermarket, we found that all fresh produce was refrigerated and that once on board, it went off within two days.

The most essential items to purchase were charts of the waterway. The Intra-Coastal Waterway (ICW) is a series of rivers and canals inter-connecting the sounds of the east coast, making a navigable waterway from Miami to New York. Another Waterway connects New York to the Great Lakes and continues via the Mississippi right down to the Gulf of Mexico. Yet another canal crosses the peninsula of Florida, making it possible to circumnavigate the whole of the eastern states with only a small area of coastal sailing in the Gulf.

We had no intention of sailing the whole of that route. Even if time and money available had not prohibited it, the fact that *Caprice* had only a small inboard motor would have made it difficult, for in places, one is moving against fairly strong currents. There are also innumerable bridges and many locks to pass through, all of which require reliable manoeuvrability.

We departed mid-week for Norfolk, the biggest city in Virginia, lying at the southern entrance to Chesapeake Bay. It was a pleasant change to sail and motor in the sheltered, tree-lined water-ways with their occasional, pretty, off-lying bays where one can anchor. We soon became used to the U.S. system of buoyage and all the channel markers which were as prolific as road signs. The port and starboard markers are the opposite to the rest of the world, where the port hand marker is kept to port on entry.

It was almost mid-summer, so the days were long and the evenings mild. However, as soon as we anchored, we discovered the wisdom of remaining in the cabin, the hatches guarded with mosquito netting. Not only mosquitoes, but also gnats and sandflies abounded. We made the most of the daylight hours, being eager to reach the Chesapeake Bay where friends were awaiting our arrival.

With the Avon dinghy semi-inflated and strapped on the deck, the helmsman had to stand and often, when the engine was running and the midday sun beating down, we had to keep water on the cockpit floor to prevent the hot fibreglass from burning our feet. We were unable to use the awning when we were moving because it interfered with ease of moving about the deck.

North of Pamlico Sound, there is an alternate route called the Dismal Swamp which, by repute, belies its name by being very attractive. We intended to take this route and anchored the second night by Elizabeth City. Next morning, we were disappointed to find that the bridge couldn't be opened due to a mechanical failure, so we had to lose a day returning to the entrance of the North Landing River, the route to Norfolk taken by the commercial traffic. We resolved to sail through the Dismal Swamp on our return.

After five days of sailing from dawn to dusk, we arrived in Norfolk and tied up at the Norfolk Yacht and Country Club. When our friends picked us up and took us to stay with them for a few days, we were whirled into 'civilisation' again. Suddenly, there were late nights, lots of gossip, people to meet and we found it all very exhausting. Jamie was alternately bewildered and fascinated until he collapsed into nervous exhaustion. There was shaggy carpet to lie on, a cat to watch, T.V. and lots of people paying him attention, not to mention the delights of a bathroom where water whooshed out of taps and the toilet made loud noises when it was flushed. We were most relieved to return to our own small world aboard *Caprice*.

Gwynn's Island, on the south western coast of the Chesapeake, was our next stopping place. This tiny island is a quiet summer holiday resort linked to the mainland by bridge. There, we left *Caprice* in the custody of Gilbert Klingel, author of *Boat Building in Steel*, while we were driven up into the Appalachian Mountains to stay for a month with friends who have a secluded, tree-covered, mountain-side home-site close to the Virginia-Tennessee border.

This young couple, whom we'd known in Sydney, had toured the world by Land-Rover before making their home in Virginia. Their daughter was only a few weeks older than Jamie, so it was a happy month we spent with them, exchanging experiences of travel and babies.

Jamie's basket which had been his cot since Durban

At the end of July, we returned to Gwynn's Island to spend the next few weeks doing boat maintenance and with the task of building a pilot berth for Jamie. He was, at ten months, able to climb out of his basket.

Ian was worried that the heat of the engine running for long hours had weakened the cockpit floor, so he reinforced and strengthened it, glassing in a layer of *Airex* foam which also served the purpose of keeping our feet a little higher than the water slopping in the cockpit drains. It was also time for anti-fouling. While Ian and I worked on *Caprice*, the dinghy sat on the grass in a shady spot and served as a playpen for Jamie, who had now learned to crawl.

At first, we'd planned to sail as far north as New York, but several events combined to end that plan. Instead, we spent a week as crew aboard a 15m junk-rigged vessel built in steel by Tom Colvin, friend of Gil Klingel and fellow author.

We visited the northern Maryland shore of Chesapeake Bay, then crossed to Annapolis before returning to *Caprice*. We liked Annapolis and decided to sail *Caprice* there for the big 'in the water', Fall Sail Boat Show.

By mid-September, we'd finished our maintenance tasks on *Caprice* and set off to sail leisurely north. Our first stop was at a small yacht club not far from Gwynn's Island where our New Zealand friends on *Ben Gunn* were staying. From there, we made overnight stops at a couple of picturesque anchorages, before reaching the South River on the outskirts of Annapolis, where some new friends, Cathy and Bill Cook, invited us to use their mooring and we stayed for a week.

Cathy was buying canned foods to stock their boat for winter in the Bahamas, and took me with her to all the supermarkets, hunting for specials. I made use of the space on their porch to varnish the cans as protection against rust.

Cathy and Bill were keen to sail with us on our boat, so we offered to take them to Annapolis, a half day trip. The day we went was completely calm and we motored the whole way. Cathy and Bill, like most Americans who came on board, were impressed with the Top Hat, even though they didn't get to actually sail on her.

Annapolis Harbour was crowded with yachts from many nations: England, Sweden, Canada, Australia, New Zealand, South Africa and France. Among them were several old friends met in the West Indies or earlier. The shore was liberally sprinkled with boat builders, repair yards, marine engineers, marinas and yacht clubs. The town itself is very old and hence geared to pedestrian shopping rather than cars.

Caprice *on slipway, USA. Shows wind steering gear
Note auxiliary rudder*

We contacted Wayne and Carole Roberts of *Landfall,* who had completed their circumnavigation and were back home in Washington D. C. preparing their boat for sale. They drove us to their flat to stay the weekend. Their baby, like ours, born in Durban, was company for Jamie, who took advantage of the floor space to start walking. Ian and Wayne sorted *Landfall's* charts and we bought from them most of the ones we needed for the Pacific. Unfortunately, our sightseeing in Washington was forestalled. A storm was forecast so we raced back to *Caprice* to find the drama already over. Gusts of 80 knots had played havoc in the crowded anchorage. Although *Caprice* hadn't dragged anchor, three other boats had dragged down on her, leaving superficial scratches in her paintwork.

We found the boat show to be very educational. In many respects, our opinions of American boats were confirmed. They are fitted out expensively, especially in the galley of the 'family cruising sailboat' to appeal to the gadget-minded woman. Underneath, there was little solidity and most 'blue water' yachts would have required considerable strengthening before they could be taken into the ocean. We inspected most of the yachts in the 11- 12m range, but found few among them that came anywhere near meeting our requirements for a family cruising yacht.

Annapolis harbour during the boat show

By the time that the boat show closed, we realised winter was coming fast. We had out all our woollen clothes again and soon decided it was time to move on. After two weeks in Annapolis, we had reached the stage of becoming entwined in inter-personal relationships. After that, the longer one stays, the more difficult it is to leave. We needed to head south.

We had one more stop-over to make. From Annapolis, we went to Poquoson near Norfolk, where an Australian girl we'd met and her American husband have a water-front home. They had asked us to visit them and we estimated that we could cross the river bar to their landing at high spring tide. Unfortunately, Ian didn't realise how long it took for the wind effect on tide to dissipate and *Caprice* ended up hard aground on the bar for twenty-four hours before the tide was sufficiently high to kedge her off again.

We stayed ashore for several days, using the sheltered space of Richard's garage to varnish the steering vane. From Poquoson, it was down to Norfolk once more for a further couple of days with our friends there. Finally, we were ready to set off south down the waterway.

Already there were frosts at night and we found *Caprice*'s unlined interior streaming with condensation each morning. We were forced to take the North Landing River route again. The summer had been so dry, the Dismal Swamp wasn't navigable.

Late in the afternoon after departing from Norfolk, we were most surprised to pass *Mithranda* in the waterway. Jenny and Bob, with their daughter Nancy, were almost home to Annapolis after a world cruise which commenced after they launched their boat in the Philippines. Unfortunately, we were not in a position to stop and a shouted greeting had to suffice for these friends we'd not seen since leaving Durban.

The tree-lined canals of Virginia and North Carolina had changed into their full autumn splendour and the water was dark with tannin and decomposed leaves. We kept on the move, starting each morning at approximately 8.00am and anchoring again before 5.00pm. The anchorages are spaced apart at a day's run so that with our little engine, we needed to leave earlier and arrive later than most of the bigger yachts in whose company we were travelling. Several of them were boats and crews we'd become acquainted with in Annapolis.

Motoring through the Intra Coastal Waterway, USA

We marked off the distance travelled by the bridges we passed through. Most are maintained by the U.S. Army Corps of Engineers. As one approaches a bridge, one blasts the fog horn three times. Usually, the bridge is opened promptly. On one occasion, we had to wait several hours while the mechanics opened the bridge by hand after the automatic mechanism failed. There was a rush of boats through the bridge, the slower ones being pushed to the edge of the channel.

There, for the first time, we were surprised to find our keel touched bottom while we were inside the marked channel. As we progressed south, this became a fairly regular occurrence. The channel was supposed to be dredged to twelve feet, but sometimes, the tugs knocked in the edge of the channel. When they grounded, they simply revved their powerful engines, leaving heaps of mud mid-channel.

Another day, when we were cold and tired, we decided to anchor in a small cul-de-sac. Before we were outside the marked edge of the main channel, we became stuck in the mud. This time, we didn't get off so easily because the tide was falling. At midnight, when the tide rose again, we had to kedge off and motor another few kilometres to the next anchorage. Trying to line up unlit markers in the dark, moonless night was a nerve-wracking task.

Navigational bridge, ICW

Just south of Charleston, we faced a slightly different problem. We were trying to negotiate a narrow cut between two natural waterways when we found the current taking us backwards at half a knot. We turned about and anchored until the strength of the current eased when the tide turned. The bottom was water-swept rock and our anchor dragged many metres before it finally held.

One Sunday, as we crossed Port Royal Sound, we were hailed from a large Coast Guard vessel and ordered to heave to. Four armed men approached in a Zodiac and one of them came aboard without even asking our permission. He demanded to see our registration papers and seemed surprised when Ian pulled out the British ship registration document. Although they claimed it to be a regular check, we suspected they were looking for a particular yacht, probably stolen and carrying drugs from South or Central America.

After we'd been travelling south for about four weeks, motoring much of the time, we discovered that the prop shaft was badly worn and consequently over-heating. With it in this state, we found that the canal in which we were travelling crossed at right angles a fairly swiftly flowing river. When we were half way across, the engine struggling to prevent *Caprice* from being carried downstream onto the rocks, a tug pushing a string of barges (this was called a tow) appeared from the other direction.

The driver seemed slightly irate that we were in his way, but if we were to have any chance of entering the canal on the other side, there was no way we could give way to him. With his powerful engines, we decided, he could go round us.

A large 'tow' in the Intracoastal Waterway

Exhausted, we pulled in at Thunderbolt marina to buy petrol and check out possibilities for the repair of the shaft. A woman greeted us, informing us that her husband was an Australian working at the marina. Was there any way in which they could help us?

Ian told her of the problem with the prop shaft, and soon we were invited to raft alongside their yacht and use the expensive marina facilities free of charge. This was typical of the hospitality we found in the States. Ian found he was able to remove the worn shaft underwater. A new one was machined, then donning his wet suit again, Ian fitted it. Due to the kindness of this couple, a potentially expensive replacement cost us only the price of the new shaft. Three days later, we were on our way again.

In Sapelo Sound, we encountered heavy fog. This was my first experience of sailing in fog and I found it quite eerie. I stood on the bow, peering to find the markers, while Ian kept close tabs on our speed, distance and direction. In such conditions, we were glad that the channel was so well marked.

We made a short stop-over in Titusville in Florida, taking a bus ride to the Kennedy Space Station on Cape Canaveral. We were disappointed to find the information directed to the intelligence level of senior primary school children.

In Florida, the vegetation was distinctly sub-tropical and there were many more waterfowl to be seen than previously. Despite the southern latitude and somewhat warmer days, it was still very cold at night, with an occasional frost.

Jamie in Florida (winter)

The last crisis we faced in the waterway occurred at West Palm Beach. We had anchored off the channel while Ian rowed ashore to find the Post Office to collect our mail. Soon after he left, I remembered that although Jamie was wearing his life jacket, he was not harnessed. As I emerged into the cockpit with the harness, I heard a splash. Jamie had fallen through the pulpit rail. I went straight over the side after him because there was a one knot current flowing. Fortunately, although it was mid-December, the water was warm from the Gulf Stream. Once I had hold of Jamie, I began to panic. How was I to get aboard again with neither dinghy nor boarding ladder?

When a boat passed down the channel, I yelled for help, but there was no visible response. I realised I had to help myself. There was no way I could stay in the water holding onto *Caprice* until Ian's return, so keeping Jamie's face out of the water, I swam to the stern and, with adrenalin running high, managed to heave myself up on the self-steering support sufficiently to push Jamie through the railing into the cockpit, then pull myself aboard. Normally, I find it extremely difficult to get aboard on my own this way.

Shaking with relief that we were safely aboard again, I stripped off our wet clothes and wrapped us both in a large dry towel. Just then, the Coast Guard vessel arrived to help. Apparently, the passing cruiser had heard my cries, but instead of stopping to help, had called the Coast Guard. They were reluctant to depart when I told them I had saved us myself. They tried to insist that we should visit a doctor. I thanked them and refused.

A few days later, we reached Miami. The last 150km had been rough. The bridges were spaced at 1/2 km intervals and the speedboat traffic was very heavy, creating a lot of wash in the narrow channels. We felt pleased we'd made the effort to travel the waterway, but we agreed it was an experience we did not wish to repeat.

Speed boats creating heavy wash in Miami

11. Christmas in the Bahamas and a Panama Transit

The Miami we saw was very different from that pictured in tourist brochures. After six months of cruising the south-eastern waterways, this was our exit port from the United States. We took a berth at the city marina rather than anchoring out, in order to facilitate official clearance procedures. These proved to be the simplest we experienced anywhere in our four years of travelling.

No officials tramped in heavy shoes on our decks. Instead, we visited the Customs Office and there, we were given a form to be stamped and returned by post from our next port. Complications arose, however, from another factor: we were not quite ready to leave when our visas expired. I spent several hours at the immigration office, pleading for an extension. We couldn't put to sea into the Gulf Stream unprepared and without favourable weather conditions. Finally, they relented and wishing the official a most happy Christmas, I clasped the extension papers and raced back to *Caprice* to relieve Ian from child minding.

One reason for our delay was the fact that our smallpox immunisation needed up-dating. Jamie, by then thirteen and a half months, was also, by World Health regulations, required to have the vaccination. We found our way to the Miami Health Department's clinic. There, to our amazement, an interpreter had to be found! All the staff was Spanish speaking in order to cater for the large number of Cubans who have migrated to Miami.

Thoughts of preparation for Christmas, a few days away, were pushed aside as *Caprice* had to be thoroughly checked over before we could put to sea again. On the afternoon of December 22nd, we gratefully escaped from the reporters and photographers who had besieged us, and motored to No Name Harbour a few miles away from the city. There, we spent a peaceful night, but next morning found the wind back in the north against the Gulf Stream. After much deliberation and a trip ashore to phone for an up-date to the weather forecast, we decided that the conditions were light enough to risk the trip across to Bimini, the closest of the Bahamian islands.

It is a 65 mile crossing, so it had to be done overnight. By the time we'd sounded our way across a shallow spit by way of a short cut to the main channel, the wind was gusting to 20 knots from ENE. Darkness was already falling and the channel was unmarked, so there was no turning back.

By evening, we were out of the lee of the land and conditions were obviously deteriorating. I was already vomiting, Ian was quite queasy and Jamie was pale too. It was his first time on the open sea since he'd learned to walk, and along with a sense of balance, he'd become susceptible to seasickness.

Ian stayed on deck changing down sails, until by 8.30p.m., we were lying to, without sail. The seas were sharp, short and disorganised. Waves were about three metres, but fortunately, most weren't steep. It was almost Christmas Eve and we had to be stuck in the notorious Gulf Stream in a busy shipping channel with a gale raging.

Pessimistic depression is a normal accompaniment of seasickness and we had our fair share that night. We estimated that the wind reached 40 knots at the height of the storm, but there was never any danger of damage to *Caprice* from the sea conditions. The threat was from ships which were passing in all directions.

Ian spent most of the night keeping watch while I comforted a frightened and miserable Jamie. At first light, Ian raised the triple-reefed main and storm jib. Conditions were slowly easing and of course the motion under sail was more comfortable. RDF (radio direction finder) checks on the beacon at Bimini reassured us that the wind had countered the current sufficiently to keep us on course.

In between bouts of vomiting, I managed to get a light breakfast for Ian and Jamie, then scramble into my water-proofs to relieve Ian at the tiller. After I'd been out there for about 20 minutes, it occurred to me to look well over the bow. To my amazement, there was Bimini! Immediately our spirits rose. The current had carried us 25-30 miles in the right direction. Conditions had been rough enough to shake away any over-confidence; to remind us that the sea is always the master and we are at its mercy.

We were both very nervous and tired. I was getting bouts of uncontrollable shaking, and since this does not normally accompany my sea-sickness, I assumed it to be an effect of the smallpox vaccination a few days previously.

There are two approaches across a sandbar into the Bimini channel. We tried for the northern one twice, but got cold feet by the time we were in soundings of two metres with close to one metre waves. The sight of a motor cruiser wrecked on the bar did nothing to increase our confidence, so we tried the longer southern approach. The approach was not an easy one, even when we followed carefully the directions in the Bahamas Sailing Guide. We had to dodge rocks and shoals, our engine struggling to make way against the strong current. Finally, we were in sheltered water and soon after receiving our cruising permit, we were relaxing at anchor.

It was Christmas Eve. Apart from buying a present for Jamie, I'd made no preparations for Christmas. We exchanged visits with the Canadian family on the only other yacht at anchor, but otherwise spent the quietest, loneliest Christmas ever.

After a couple of days, we moved south to Gunn Cay where we anchored over-night on the eastern side of the island. There, Ian found several conchs while swimming, so we decided to try this famous Bahamian delicacy. Following the directions given in the Cruising Guide, it took us three and a half hours to prepare them. However, when we developed more expertise in removing the fish from its shell, conch fritters tasted just as delicious as that first time.

On Boxing Day, we set off to cross the Grand Bahama Bank. What a strange section of sea! The bottom is flat and sandy, and at three metres, always visible. We sailed all day. Then, well out of the sight of land, anchored for the night; an act which reminded us of those land-lubberly questions: "What do you do at night? Anchor?"

The next night, we anchored within sight of the light structure which is situated close to the eastern side of the bank. There was no hope of reaching Nassau the next day, so we pulled into an anchorage at Francis Hogg Cay, where we enjoyed roaming the deserted beach, gathering shells and more conchs. This was one of many privately owned islands in the Bahamas where the big house is used only for vacations. The rest of the year it is left in the charge of a caretaker. We remained at that lovely anchorage for several days, including New Year.

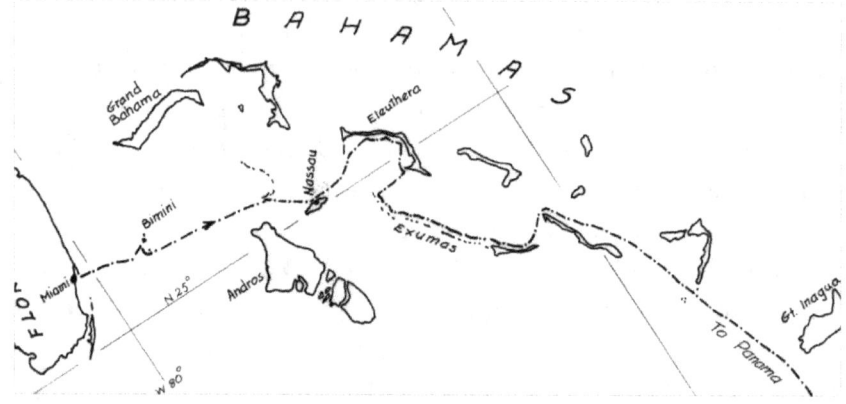

Route through the Bahamas

On a beautifully clear, almost calm day, we drifted across to Nassau under spinnaker, entering the harbour at sunset. The Bahamas being a member of the British Commonwealth, we had expected to find a certain amount of British influence, especially in products on sale. However, we hadn't taken sufficient account of the fact that the chief industry is catering to the American tourist.

Upon our return to *Caprice* after touring the city, we were delighted to find *Ben Gunn* anchored nearby. Kevin and Tony built their fibreglass H28 in Wellington, New Zealand, and we first met them in Durban and later in several other ports. We spent the rest of the day catching up on news of mutual friends. Soon, we had decided to cruise the rest of the Bahamian islands in their company.

A couple of days later, both yachts moved out of New Providence to make our way towards Eleuthera. We spent our nights in quiet anchorages and nearly every day, stopped early to swim, dive, snorkel or look for shells. Sailing around small islands in shallow waters was a very different experience from either ocean sailing, the water-ways of the USA or even the West Indies. Here, we rapidly learned to sail with the sun over our shoulders, so that we could recognise the depth by the water colour.

One afternoon, after being caught in a strange current and unable to make headway, Ian cut a corner in his haste to make anchor before dusk. I was busy bringing in the fishing line when we suddenly found ourselves just bumping bottom in the very light swell. We motored on in 1.5m of water, dodging clumps of grass (difficult to differentiate from rocks) until we were back in the channel.

Next morning, we found our anchor dragging when the tide changed, so we decided to move on. As we rounded the end of that island, appropriately named 'Current Island', the tide was with us, but we had quite a strong head wind. The channel was very narrow and close to the shore. At one point, the water became so turbulent, the tiller refused to answer. *Caprice* began to turn broadside as the current took us past the rocks with only a narrow margin. Within minutes, we were on the leeward side of the island and able to breathe easily again.

After departing from Governor's Harbour in Eleuthera, we anchored off Powell Point at the southern end of that island, before crossing the 25 miles of deep water to the Exuma chain. Our anchorage that night was quite exposed and the wind was fairly strong. Whenever the wind eased, the tidal current swung *Caprice* viciously in the opposite direction. Since the holding is poor in most Bahamian anchorages, we were in the habit of setting both anchors "V" style from the bow. With the sharp swinging, one line caught round the rudder, exposing it to abnormal stress. We didn't realise the rudder had been damaged until we set sail the next day, when the tiller behaved oddly.

We reached our next anchorage, Highborne Cay, without difficulty and there Ian dived to check out the rudder. He found that the fibreglass had broken away from the top of the rudder where the stock enters. Our dismay was short-lived when Tony realised that he'd been given a letter of introduction to the manager of this very island.

The manager was keen to offer assistance and allowed Ian full use of his large, well equipped workshop which contained a welder. Two days later, with a heavy strap welded to the stock, bolted to the blade and glassed over, we had a much stronger rudder.

Our next anchorage was at Norman's Cay. At 4.00 a.m., the frontal system of a huge depression (centred over Bermuda) began moving across the Bahamas. It brought freezing conditions and gale force winds with gusts in excess of 50 knots. Our particular anchorage had good holding but, according to the news report, it was chaotic elsewhere. In Nassau, three inter-island vessels sank. Snow fell on Grand Bahama and in Miami. Such a storm had never before been recorded in the area.

We visited a couple more cays in the Exuma chain before heading to Stocking Island opposite Georgetown, the largest town outside of Nassau. There, we were delighted to be greeted by Cathy and Bill Cook, with whom we'd stayed at Chesapeake Bay. In Georgetown, we shopped for groceries fuel and water in preparation for our passage down to Panama. After four days at Stocking Island, we said farewell to Cathy and Bill, and also to Kevin and Tony, who intended to visit Haiti, before returning to the USA.

Without calling at any of the south eastern islands of the Bahamas, we sailed down to the Windward Passage which passes between Haiti and Cuba, then set course directly for Panama. Sailing conditions were mild until we were through the Windward Passage, when the trade winds came in on the beam. From there on, we made excellent time, covering an average of 130 miles a day.

The motion was uncomfortable until the wind moved further astern, and the spray meant we had to keep the hatches closed, but by way of compensation, the self-steering handled *Caprice* admirably at six and a half knots.

Ten hours before we reached the Canal Zone, the auxiliary rudder snapped, but we managed to salvage the pieces. It was no real hardship to steer *Caprice* those last few miles. We followed a merchant ship through the breakwater into Limon Bay, an oiler coming up astern.

We felt a mixture of trepidation and audacity at bringing *Caprice* into the Canal Zone. This was designed for big ships! Then a pilot boat approached us and with a cheerful greeting, the officer handed us a packet of papers, forms and a guide specifically prepared for yachtsmen. We were being treated as though we had every right to be there! We anchored *Caprice* where we were directed and the formalities were promptly taken care of.

Since *Caprice* had never been through the canal before, she had to be "admeasured" so that charges could be calculated according to her "tonnage". The sum was ridiculously low considering that we had a pilot aboard for twelve hours.

Prior to the transit, we moved to the yacht club at Cristobal. From there, I visited Colon City in Panama. It was the most depressingly poverty-stricken city I have ever seen and I was grateful that the taxi driver elected himself as my bodyguard while I shopped. It was quite unsafe for me to walk unescorted.

Looking back into Gatun Lock

At 7.00 a.m., we were ready to enter the first lock behind the ship with which we shared the transit. The canal consists of three locks up to Lake Gatun, the lake itself, Galliard Cut, then Pedro Miguel lock, Mira Flores (another small lake) and the two Mira Flores locks down to the Pacific. We were grateful that our pilot was also a sailor, for some pilots insist on motoring across the lake. Without the extra speed under sail, *Caprice* would have been behind schedule for the downward locks.

Motoring through the Gaillard Cut

We motored through The Galliard Cut, the seven miles of canal cut through the continental divide, then passed down Pedro Miguel lock and across the Mira Flores lake. After a minor accident in which Ian was injured at Pedro Miguel, we were pleased to pass through the Mira Flores locks without incident.

It was dusk by the time we reached our mooring at the Balboa Yacht club. After three years, we were in the Pacific again. It was time to make preparations for our crossing to French Polynesia.

The gates opening for us to leave Pedro Miguel Lock

Ship Entering Mira Flores Lock behind us

12 The Pacific: Homeward Bound

The ordeal of the Panama Canal transit behind us, we were able to think ahead to the Pacific crossing and preparations for it. Our request for permission to cruise the Galapagos Islands in *Caprice* was refused, so we decided not to stop there at all. Instead, we planned to visit Stevenson's uninhabited Treasure Island, Cocos, before making the long 4,000 mile crossing to the Marquesas, the eastern-most group of French Polynesia. We knew that this passage would be our longest and that we could be out of reach of normal food supplies for more than two months if we met adversely light conditions.

This time, we had the additional problem of provisioning for Jamie. I weaned him while we were in Panama, so I had to take large quantities of powdered milk along. This placed an extra burden on our fresh water supplies. However, we knew we would be able to top up the tank at Cocos Island and also during squalls in the doldrums.

To gain permission to anchor at the small Panamanian island of Taboga, it is necessary to visit the maritime authority's office in Panama City to obtain a *Zarpe*. Although Panama City has the gay, pulsating South American atmosphere lacking in Colon, crime is rife there too. Whilst the Americans employ as many Panamanians as they can in the Canal Zone, out of the zone, unemployment is extremely high so that maybe as much as one fifth the adult population sustains itself by picking pockets.

Taboga (the Island of Flowers) lies only a few miles from Balboa Yacht Club, It is a preferred haven for cruising yachts. Being the official show-place for visiting dignitaries, the island is kept free of pickpockets and criminals. For yachtsmen, the anchorage is free and with a tidal range of nearly six metres, it makes an excellent place to anti-foul the hull.

On Saturday evening, while anchored at Taboga, a carnival for a pre-Lent festival was in full swing. The ferry boat, laden with very merry visitors, cut across our mooring line, catching the anchor-marker line in its propeller. Suddenly, we found ourselves being towed shore-wards at five knots behind the ferry. When the ferry stopped at the jetty, Ian had to get in the dinghy, cut the line, retrieve the anchor, then, rowing as hard as he could, tow *Caprice* back to a safe anchorage. By the time that little adventure was over, we were in no mood for going ashore to join in the festivities.

After a week in Taboga, we felt ready to set off again. Ian had painted the hull between tides; he'd fixed the broken voltage regulator; I'd varnished the woodwork and topped up our stores with eight dozen really fresh eggs, which I coated in Vaseline for long-term protection.

We got under way just before midday on February 23, sailing south through the Gulf of Panama under light conditions, until the sea breeze freshened for several hours in the evening. About 10 pm, we were becalmed and when I went forward to drop the headsail, a school of dolphins was frolicking at the bow. It was a truly incredible sight to see their complete forms aglow with brilliant bio-luminescence.

Bird life was also prolific in the gulf. We were entranced to see pelicans flying in formation, then, sighting a school of fish, they dived in concert. Frigate Birds soared high above.

Before sunset the second night, a healthy 2kg mackerel took the hook of our fishing line – just in time for dinner. Delicious! It is the cold Humboldt Current sweeping up the South American coast that attracts so much marine life in this area.

By our third day at sea, when we were clear of Punta Mala and out of the gulf, Ian altered course to the west of Cocos. This took us well clear of all the major shipping routes. After seven days, we sighted the island and were surprised to see an 18m junk-rigged vessel at anchor there. The island is normally uninhabited and infrequently visited.

The *Richmond* had arrived the previous afternoon, forty eight days out of San Francisco. En route to Costa Rica, they had been blown off course by a gale and then becalmed. Running low on water, the skipper had decided to put in at Cocos Island before proceeding to Costa Rica. This proved a providential decision, for living on the island they found a young family who wanted passage to Costa Rica before the imminent birth of their next child. Juan Fernandez, his pregnant wife and child had lived on Cocos for six months after being evicted from the Galapagos.

Wild pig, deer, fish and coconuts are abundant and this diet they supplemented with fruit and vegetables from their own garden. The garden was originally established by the most persistent of the many treasure hunters to visit Cocos — a German who lived a hermit existence there for eight years.

We remained at Cocos for three days after the *Richmond* departed with the Fernandez family, delighting in this luxuriant paradise. We gathered coconuts, guavas and limes, swam in the fresh water and Ian dived with his spear gun to catch fish.

We reluctantly raised anchor and set out on the next leg. Soon, we found ourselves amid floating logs, sawn planks and other debris. We motored on, dodging the largest branches until the propeller stopped and we found a length of old polypropylene rope wound around it. Unable to free it from on board, once again Ian had to dive. The sun was low in the sky before we were clear of the island. (The garbage collects in this convergence area of several currents which now, in 2012, covers several square miles.)

After leaving Cocos, we spent many days in the doldrums. The water temperature was 22°C, the air temperature about 30°C and the humidity very high. The deck became too hot to walk on. Progress in this area of the Pacific was extremely slow. Seven days passed before we sighted the nearest island of the Galapagos group and another three of travelling vaguely south, before we found some wind, albeit intermittent.

The water became slightly cooler and once again we saw evidence of more prolific marine life. One hot, still afternoon, a large turtle bumped around the hull for half an hour before it swam off, its shell newly anti-fouled.

A few days later, two whales visited. They were each about 12m in length. Because we were in the area where the Robinsons' and the Baileys' yachts were sunk by whales, I became extremely nervous, my fear communicating itself to Jamie. Nevertheless, the huge beasts just looked us over then went on their way.

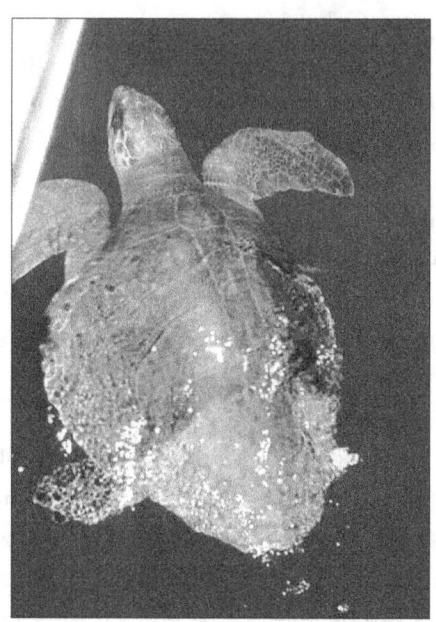

A Galapagos turtle anti-fouls its shell from our hull

On March 25 1977, 18 days out of Cocos, we found the trade winds at last. Since leaving Taboga, we'd been at sea for 25 days and in that time, covered only one third of our course to the Marquesas. We'd caught only two fish, one of which went bad and the fresh fruit and vegetables had either been eaten or gone off. Jamie was drinking more milk than I'd estimated and we found ourselves using more water than ever before, despite the fact that we used it strictly for personal consumption. As much as possible, I used salt water in cooking and Ian, in that climate, chose to grow a beard rather than shave in salt water.

Despite the care I'd taken in provisioning, our supplies were rapidly dwindling. I began to worry that we would run out of staple items if our progress did not improve. But of course, it did improve and soon we were making daily runs of 120 and 130 miles, so that by the time we reached the Marquesas, our average day's run for the 3,600 miles was 89 miles. Nevertheless, we were completely out of flour and milk powder when we finally arrived.

One day, Ian decided to measure how much water was left – about 70 litres, he concluded. We were still about 500 miles from land, so each time there was a squall we'd rush out with the buckets and collect a few litres. Then Ian decided to pour one of the two jerry cans into the tank. That was when we discovered that one of the cans had developed a leak. We had 20 litres less than we'd thought. Fortunately, over the next couple of days, we managed to collect about 50 litres by hanging a bucket at the goose-neck and taking greater care with the water-pipe leading from the cockpit awning.

After 41 days at sea, and exactly two months since leaving Taboga, we anchored at Hiva Oa, eastern-most port of entry in the Marquesas, French Polynesia. A crew member from another boat swam over to greet us. As he climbed aboard, Jamie screamed in terror. For two months, the only swimming creatures he'd seen over the side were dolphins and whales! He was very wary of other people for several days, but two other small children on yachts in the bay helped him thaw, as well as a few hours ashore chatting with the villagers. That evening, we gorged ourselves on fresh fruit.

Next day, we sailed to the island of Niku Hiva where we stayed for a week at Taiohae Bay, the main harbour for the whole group. Although this was a calm anchorage, a pretty bay and had the advantage of a fresh water shower near the landing, we were reluctant to stay. The tiniest scratch rapidly became infected, and if not treated immediately, soon developed into a tropical ulcer. The cause of these infections, we were told, was the coral polyps in the water. If the infection took hold, the only way to treat it was with tetracycline. I was concerned for Jamie who was scratching crazily at his bites. Mosquitoes and nonos (tiny sandflies) are prolific.

Tetracycline is unsuitable for young children and ampicillin didn't control the infection. Every skin lesion I could find, I painted with iodine until we were spotted all over. There were so many people sick on the boats around us that we decided to move on, despite the fact that Ian too, had a skin infection.

The Marquesas had not impressed us favourably. In the two main villages, the natives were indifferent to visitors. After two months isolation, we found re-establishing inter-personal relationships difficult, especially when we were faced with a foreign language as well. The locals speak a Polynesian dialect, but they learn French in school. Moreover, the authorities had granted us only a one month permit to reach Tahiti, 800 miles to the west, so we passed by any other islands in this group.

Between the Marquesas and Tahiti lie the Tuamotus or Dangerous Archipelago. This chain of islands consists of low lying coral atolls and reefs, around which flow unpredictable currents. The southern portion of the area is prohibited to yachts, for that is the French nuclear testing area, Muraroa.

Once again, the trade winds were fluky and it took seven days to cover the 500 miles to Ahé, the atoll where we intended to stop. After the first couple of days, navigation became Ian's chief concern. He took star sights morning and evening as well as a noon sight every day. We had no desire to add *Caprice* to the statistics of yachts wrecked in these waters.

One evening, Ian declared our position to be ten to twelve miles east of Manihi, the island next to Ahé. Soon after, we were able to see the moonlit silhouette of coconut palms through the binoculars. Once he'd confirmed our position, Ian relaxed, took down sail and went to bed.

I took over worrying. For three hours, I fussed about with the hand bearing compass, checking for any drift from current. Even when Ian came back on watch, I couldn't relax and sleep. At dawn, we were six miles off the outlying reef.

Next morning, conditions were squally, so we sailed when there was wind and motored during the calms in order to reach the entrance through the reef to Ahé at the best time – between tides and while the sun was still overhead, so we could see any coral heads.

Our timing was perfect. We found the narrow entrance and with me at the bow, lead line in hand, we eased our way across the coral into the lagoon. There, a friendly young man in a local fishing boat approached us and gestured that he would come aboard to assist us across the lagoon to the village.

Safely at anchor, we looked about and counted twelve cruising yachts at anchor. Another boat arrived a couple of days later. We found out that Bernard Moitessier had *Joshua* tucked away in the lagoon. Although we saw his boat, we didn't see him at all. He was very reclusive.

Anchorage within the lagoon at Ahé

A fishing hut on the reef at Ahé

The villagers at Ahé have a reputation for hospitality, which in reality exceeded all expectation. A population of less than 50 adults provided a feast on the Saturday night for 38 visitors!

We were invited to share in village activities such as community singing after the Sunday evening service and helping the women and children with weeding the roadways while the men went out to tend the coconuts or fish.

Mama Fana, wife of the mayor, taught us girls how to weave coconut fronds into baskets and hats. Any surplus fish, bread or coconuts were generously shared with the yachties. These lovable people had little else. It was difficult to leave such an hospitable island, but we had to get to Papéèté or risk the disapproval of the authorities. We had stayed thirteen days, so now we had to sail without the moon.

Mama Fana teaching us to make hats and baskets

The time to navigate the passage out of the lagoon depended on the tide. Thus, we were forced to negotiate the narrow passage between Rangiaroa and Arutua. After dark, none of the atolls is lit and although there is a radio aero beacon on Rangiaroa, it was of little use. That night, it was very disconcerting to be able to smell the shore, so we spent a tense night straining our ears for the sound of surf. At daylight, we were safely in the middle of the passage and by the next night, clear of all land.

It is hard to believe we could make a slower passage than those already experienced in the Pacific, but we did. One day, we found the current had actually taken us 30 miles backwards, so that 280 mile crossing took six days, an average of only 45 miles per day. How elusive Tahiti seemed when we could see its twin peaks over the horizon for two full days.

In Papéèté, we joined the other hundred or so visiting yachts lining the waterfront of that bustling, cosmopolitan, tourist city. The majority was American, but a dozen other nations were also represented among boats as diverse as one could imagine.

Tahiti, the island of love, the tiaré flower, one time home of Paul Gaugin, lies at the head of the mountainous chain known as the Society Islands. In Papéèté, the capital of French Polynesia, our second child was conceived and the rest of the voyage was greatly affected by my pregnancy.

The American yachts all celebrated the fourth of July with shore side barbeques, to which the rest of us were invited. For three weeks we attended to chores in Papéèté, before escaping to neighbouring Moorea, an island of magic and beauty which, like many of the Society Islands, beguiled us into lengthening our intended stay

On the return two mile crossing to Papéèté, I was first afflicted with the pregnancy nausea which plagued me all the way back to Australia.

Jamie on the beach at Moorea

Just as Papéèté was winding itself up for the 14th of July festivities (Bastille Day), we left for Huahine, where we hoped to enjoy the celebrations on a smaller, village scale. Unfortunately, it rained every day which spoiled a number of events, but we did get to see the team dancing competition, which was especially memorable.

Also very memorable was the arrival of "Tongan Bill" in his 5m Tucker design yacht. This delightfully outgoing Tongan built *Mata Moana* in Auckland, then set sail for Tahiti via Rarotonga, capital of the Cook Islands. En route, the boat was rolled twice. Yet another storm blew him too far north, so he made his landfall at Huahine instead of the official port of entry, Papéèté.

On a clear day, Raiatea is visible from Huahine. Within the same fringing reef, lies Tahaa. Anchorages are mostly very deep, so the technique is to find a large coral head upon which to drop the anchor. This we did outside a small village on Tahaa. There, our welcome into the village was almost as friendly as at Ahé. The traditional lifestyle was followed still. No roads linked this village with the next, so there were no vehicles. About the only visible link with modern life were the outboard motors on the fishing canoes.

The Tahaa netball team wanted to adopt Jamie

A week later, we moved on to Bora Bora, perhaps the most spectacular island in the group. Here too, especially near the main village, the anchorages average 30 metres deep. We decided to explore the north-western side of the island. To reach it, we had to wend our way between reefs, coral heads and across shallows within the lagoon until we were anchored in the lee of a motu.

All too soon, we found our visas nearly expired. The Society Islands had, temporarily at least, dispelled our homesickness. We were looking forward to Rarotonga, the last of the Pacific islands on our itinerary.

At Rarotonga, we were greeted with a most welcome gift of fresh fruit from Australian friends on *Matatua*, first met in the Post Office in Papéèté. Other friends in the harbour were Nick, and Ann Reeves, with their two boys on *Golden Opportunity*, a Golden Hind. They were migrating from the UK to Australia.

Anchor lines form a cobweb at Raratonga

We visited some places of interest – especially the place of departure for the migration of Maoris in voyaging canoes, which sailed to the Bay of Plenty, New Zealand, probably in the mid-14th century.

From Rarotonga, we tried to sail directly to New Zealand. By the time we'd beaten to windward for 27 days out of the 31 it took to reach Whangerei, we knew why the other yachts going to N.Z. sailed via Tonga. During the voyage, we had numerous pressure systems pass over. The wind would start moderately from the south west (our heading) for up to a day, and over the next several days, slowly ease off to about five knots by the time it reached our stern quarter – Caprice's ideal sailing wind. A day or so later, the pattern would be repeated. We took thirty three days to complete that leg.

Our arrival was almost premature. Picking our way across the foggy Hauraki Gulf towards the mouth of the Whangarei River, we were keeping track of our position by sailing from island to island. Ian came below to drink a cup of soup, then re-emerging on deck found himself, to his horror, looking up a cliff. He swung *Caprice* onto the opposite tack, taking her clear of the rocks 200m away.

New Zealand is where my family lives and they, of course, had not yet met Jamie. *Caprice* was left safely in the Town Basin at Whangarei, while we travelled south for a family gathering.

Later, we explored the beautiful Bay of Islands before tackling the Tasman. After our attempt to reach Lord Howe Island four years before, we anticipated the worst for this final passage. Instead, as if it wished to show us another face, the Tasman crossing was one of our most pleasant. The weather excelled itself, maintaining very favourable sailing conditions.

Only eleven days after we'd cleared Cape Maria Van Dieman, we were within sight of Newcastle. As though reluctant to let our voyage end, the wind dropped right off and we drifted slowly south through the night until early on the morning of Sunday 20th November, we motored through the heads of Port Jackson and into Watson Bay to await Customs.

*Ian and Jamie on Caprice at the CYCA Sydney
(The flags represent all the countries we have visited.)*

Passage Times in Days

Sydney (4.02.74)	to Port Noarlunga (SA)	15
Port Noarlunga	to Fremantle (Indian Ocean)	16
Fremantle	to **Rodrigues**	38
Rodrigues	to Mauritius	4
Mauritius	to **Durban (RSA)**	22
Durban	to Cape Town	8
Cape Town	to St Helena (Sth Atlantic)	17
St Helena	to Ascension	24
Cruising West Indies to North Atlantic		50
St Bartholomy	to **Morehead City (USA)**	12
Intra-Coastal-Waterway (ICW), Eastern USA		6 months
Morehead City	to Chesapeake Bay (north)	
Chesapeake Bay	to Miami (south)	
Miami	to **Bimini (Bahamas)**	overnight

1977

Islands of the Bahamas, south to Stocking Island		35
Stocking Island	to **Colon (Panama)**	9

Transit of Panama Canal 10th Feb 1977 (Pacific Ocean)

Panama City	to Taboga I (Panama)	1
Taboga I	to **Cocos Island (Costa Rica)**	7
Cocos Island	to **Marquesas (Fr. Polynesia)**	41
Marquesas	to Ahe (Tuamotu Archipelago	10
Ahe	to Papéété (Tahiti)	6
Tahiti, Moorea, Raiatea, Tahaa, Boro Bora:		2 months
Bora Bora	to **Rarotonga (Cook Islands)**	8
Rarotonga	to **Whangarei (NZ)**	33
Whangarei	to Opua	1
Opua	to Whangaroa	1
Whangaroa	to **Sydney** (20.11.77)	13

The voyage lasted 3 years, 10 months: Total Passage Days 293 + approx. 138 cruising = ~ 431 days at sea.

Part Three

Cover Article, Women's Day: August 1987

Jan Mitchell

The Baby who Sailed 20,000 Miles

This is the story of Jamie Mitchell who, at the age of two, has sailed more than half-way around the world. The son of Jan and Ian Mitchell of Sydney, his mother tells his tale.

To cross oceans in a 7.6-metre fibreglass yacht is far from most people's ideal way to travel. Until Jamie was two years old, that was the only way of life he knew. By the time he was six months old, he was a seasoned sailor, having crossed the South Atlantic Ocean from Cape Town to Barbados in the West Indies.

Jan and Ian standing on deck

Ian and I met in Sydney not long after we each completed our Bachelor degrees – Ian in Engineering at Sydney University and me in Sociology and English at Canterbury University, New Zealand. Ian was Sydney-born and had dreamed for many years of sailing the world in his own boat. Eighteen months after our marriage we bought *Caprice* and, soon after, his dream began to come true – though not on his own, as he had originally intended.

We left Pittwater, Sydney, on February 5, 1974, sailing south round the bottom of Australia to Perth. From there we crossed the Indian Ocean via Mauritius to Durban, South Africa. When Ian and I planned our circumnavigation we intended to return to Australia before having a family; instead, three months after arriving home, we were the parents of two boys.

Financial circumstances forced us to stay in South Africa for 17 months. Having coped sufficiently well with sailing from Sydney to Durban (that is, not being a member of that very small group who remain permanently seasick when at sea), I decided that motherhood at sea would reduce the number of years I'd need to be away from lucrative employment on land. With great care we planned the timing of Jamie's conception. We had to balance my term of employment against the age at which we considered we could handle sailing with a young baby. Three months, I felt, was the youngest at which I was prepared to take him to sea. Miraculously, the planning worked! I completed a full year's employment before Jamie's birth and he was just three months old when we set out across the Atlantic.

Six weeks before *Caprice*'s departure, we moved from our Durban flat to live on board again. What a hectic six weeks it was! Nappy washing at the launderette had to be fitted in between shopping for stores, feeds, varnishing, post-natal exercises, making new awnings and weekly visits to the baby clinic

Fortunately, during this busy time, Jamie was a relatively easy baby to care for. He rarely cried or objected to being wheeled all over town. Best of all, from the age of five weeks he slept at night from dusk to dawn. My chief problem resulted from a decision to demand-feed him. He had never developed a regular schedule of his own, so I couldn't predict feed times. Of course, this didn't matter later on when we were sailing. Without refrigeration, breast feeding is easiest (not to mention best for baby), but in port when we were very busy, occasions arose when I wished Ian could give him a bottle.

Laundry, including baby clothes fills the cockpit

From Durban, we decided that Jamie and I should travel overland to Cape Town, leaving Ian, with the help of two teenage lads, to sail *Caprice* down the treacherous South-East coast with its busy shipping lanes. I knew I couldn't cope with both watch-taking and breast-feeding at that stage, and *Caprice* was too small to accommodate extra crew as well as ourselves.

Our old Volkswagen, in which we had toured the Kruger National Park, was loaded and the same morning that *Caprice* began to push her bows southward, Jamie and I also started off. Nine days later we were reunited in Cape Town. Despite my fears of bad seas and weather, Ian had had good sailing conditions. He was equally relieved to find that the old Kombi had given me no trouble.

When we stepped back on board, little Jamie, then 10 weeks old, looked all around him and grinned widely. *Home again!* he seemed to be saying. That he should recognise his surroundings after 12 days' absence simply staggered me.

During the four weeks that we spent in Cape Town, familiar sights were *Caprice* bedecked with nappies and me hurrying about the yacht club grounds with Jamie slung over my shoulder. That month passed very quickly, the many chores interspersed with sightseeing about the Cape. Getting Jamie's birth certificate, passport, Australian citizenship, visa for the USA and his first injections caused many hassles, but eventually we were ready for sea again.

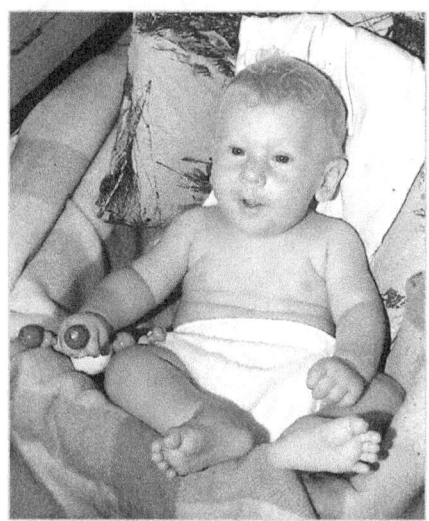

Jamie with his Mary Lou, a NZ wooden toy

Jamie was unusually fractious the day we left. Naturally, our tensions had been transmitted to him. He was well aware, even at three and a half months, that something unusual was happening, and let me know very definitely that he didn't approve of the different motion, strange noises and the vibration of the engine as we motored clear of the other vessels in the harbour.

Seasickness usually affects both Ian and me at the beginning of a passage, especially if conditions are at all rough. The doctor had assured us that Jamie would not be affected. A. widely accepted theory of seasickness is that motion at sea upsets fluid in the middle ear, centre of our balance mechanism. Although a young baby has no sense of balance, he will still get upset if his mother is feeling miserable or if dehydration from vomiting reduces her milk supply. Fortunately, this time my initial queasiness was gone within hours and Jamie's milk supply continued to flow adequately. I like to think that this was due as much to the precautions I had learned to take – every sailor has his or her own remedy for seasickness – as to the fact that we met no bad weather.

Eventually, in that first few hours at sea, Jamie settled down for the night. The engine had been switched off some hours before and the more regular motion under sail no longer worried him. The self-steering gear was set to work and Ian and I began to relax as we fell into our familiar routines. I started wondering about Jamie again, fervently hoping that I could cope. Living on board a yacht with a baby was one thing in port, but at sea? One has to be completely self-reliant there. Should he get sick, there would be no doctor or hospital to help, so I had acquired medicines for the most common baby ailments. Little did I know how thankful I would be later for those medications.

A more immediate problem was how Jamie's tender skin would react to sea-water baths and sea-water washed nappies. Perhaps we'd have enough fresh water in which to sponge bath him. *Caprice* carries 230 litres of fresh water, and on an ocean crossing this is normally reserved entirely for personal consumption. Hair-washing, shaving, laundry, all else is done in sea water. I remembered seeing Ian with the water hose on deck earlier in the day.

'Ian, you did fill the jerry cans as well as the water tank, didn't you'?'

'Did I fill the tank? I thought you had!'

'But when I saw you with the hose, I asked if you had done the water. Didn't you say yes?'

'I said no. All I did was fill the cans.'

How much water did we have? Would we have to turn back? I knew Ian would be very reluctant to do so. Fortunately, it was only two days since I had filled the tank, but we had intended to top it up before departing. How much had I used in that time? In port, we use water freely. Ian carefully measured the level in the tank. It was down 15cm. That was about 25 litres. Our next port, St Helena, was nearly 3000 kilometres away and the chance of sufficient rain to catch water was slight in that area of the Atlantic. More important, would the landing conditions at St Helena be calm enough to enable us to transport jerry cans of water?

Jamie, you had better not get salt-water rash, I thought. Much to my relief as we sailed on, his skin seemed to be unaffected by the salt water. For three months his bath was in sea water. Baby soap will not lather in it, so instead I washed him in the same cheap detergent-based shampoo that Ian and I used. His nappies and clothes, too, were washed in sea water. I used soap only if the napkin was stained and rinsed them all very thoroughly.

Provided Jamie was changed regularly and received a daily sunbathe, he got no rash. To begin with I was also worried that his fair skin would burn easily, especially with the salt on his skin, but he seems to have inherited my slowness to burn or tan. Despite sunning sessions for as much as 40 minutes daily on the upturned dinghy on deck, he didn't burn and only now, at the age of two, is developing much of a tan.

Jamie and Ian on Deck, Nappies Fluttering above

The washing of other clothes for Jamie and ourselves became less of a problem as we moved further north into the tropics. By the time we reached St Helena, it was rarely cool enough for Jamie to need even a vest at night. Drying clothes is more of a problem on *Caprice* than on larger yachts where the railing is much higher above the water and spray. We solved this problem by sewing tapes on two corners of each nappy and making special loops on a halyard (rope) which was rigged half- way up the mast. We tied on three or four nappies at a time and hauled them above the spray, where they fluttered like large white flags. Usually the nappies were soft and dry enough after a couple of hours, even in the humidity. It was probably those nappies fluttering from the halyard that caused us our biggest fright during the entire Atlantic crossing.

Ian and I were in the cockpit, leisurely eating lunch and enjoying a break from Jamie, who was asleep inside, when I spotted a ship. We estimated its course in relation to ours. It seemed that the ship should pass nearly half a mile to starboard of us. At the time there was very little wind, so we were not in a position to manoeuvre easily under sail. Feeling slightly uneasy, we turned on the petrol and batteries ready to start the engine in case of emergency. Sure enough, when the ship was abeam of *Caprice*, it turned and started moving directly towards us, apparently investigating the flapping nappies.

The Hellenic ideal approaches much too close

I began to panic. It's not that we don't appreciate someone checking that we are okay; the problem is that many ships' captains don't understand how to come safely alongside a sailing vessel. We know of yachts which have smashed part of their masts and rigging against the side of a large ship which has come too close to allow the sailing vessel to manoeuvre.

Ian tried to start the engine. As usual, when we really needed it, it didn't start. The ship was still steering straight for us, her bow pointed amidships. It was coming very close. My teeth started chattering with fright. I was visualising myself grabbing Jamie and jumping overboard. That ship was going to inadvertently ram us, I was certain.

'There's nothing we can do, so l might as well take a photo,' said Ian in a voice that seemed so calm. By now l was too petrified to move. Then, perhaps 300 metres away the ship began to turn, still skidding through the water towards us.

At that moment, the captain blasted his horn three times in greeting. Poor little Jamie, blissfully asleep until then, opened his eyes and screamed in terror. In two bounds, I was below, cradling him in my arms. Through the window, the ship was still visible and I was shaking uncontrollably with relief that they had turned just in time. I took Jamie into the cockpit with me, where l could brace myself firmly against the severe rocking which I knew was soon to follow as the *Hellenic Ideal* cut across our bows, leaving a large wake.

Just four days after our encounter with the *Hellenic Ideal* the lovely island of St Helena came into view. We had made excellent time, covering an average of 165 kilometres a day. As with our departure from Cape Town, our tensions and excitement transmitted themselves to Jamie. At the time, I attributed his grumpiness to sore gums and teething, but his upsets came to be a problem I soon associated with entering and leaving ports. Close to land, while Ian was busy with the anchor and chain, l would have to steer and Jamie would lie, complaining, in his cot just inside the companionway. Trying to keep *Caprice* on course while l comforted Jamie by crooning (out of tune), 'Hush little baby, don't you cry...' was a difficult task. Inevitably, l would let the wind back the sails, earning myself a strongly worded reprimand from Ian. How I wished there was some safe way I could have our baby sitting up in the cockpit where he could watch us both when we were busy.

Sitting Jamie up at any time during those three months proved more of a problem than I had anticipated. He had always been an alert, curious and wakeful little boy during daylight hours, taking no more than an hour's nap morning and afternoon. Naturally, he hated to be left lying on his back where he couldn't see what was going on. How I regretted my decision not to buy one of those cheap plastic baby chairs. Propping him up with cushions was no solution on the yacht when we were under sail. By four and a half months he was trying to sit himself up, so that one lurch of the boat, or even an injudicious wriggle on his part, caused him to topple and hit his face on the edge of the cot, at the same time contriving to land his ribs atop a hard toy. Anything I used to pad the edges of the cot he promptly removed and chewed. Nor could I put him on the floor when there are only two square metres of floor space.

Ashore in Barbados was the first time Jamie had a steady floor to sit on. He looked so puzzled when it didn't move, we couldn't help laughing. We were able to bring out the back carry-pack we had been given in Durban. Now, at six and a half months, Jamie's back was strong enough for him to sit up for two hours at a time, gaining a bird's-eye view of his surroundings, not only ashore but also on board where we had devised a method of holding his seat upright.

Also in Barbados, Jamie had his third three-in-one injection and oral polio vaccine. He had had the first dose before we left Cape Town and the second in St Helena. He would receive his next lot of shots in the United States.

It was at St Bartholomew (known as St Barts), in the French West Indies, that Jamie fell sick. We had left the island for the USA before I realised his symptoms could not be attributed to teething. (He had already cut four teeth since our arrival in the West Indies, and another two were trying to make an appearance.).

After five days of worsening diarrhoea and fretfulness but no new tooth, Jamie's condition began to worry me. What I had assumed to be reaction to heat and humidity became obvious as chronic fever. Feelings of guilt beset I me. How could I have neglected to notice that my baby was sick? Worse, his fretting had made me bad-tempered with him.

I consulted Dr Spock: *'In the olden days it was the custom to blame teeth for colds, diarrhoeas, fevers. Of course, these diseases are caused by germs and not teething'* I went through the medicine cabinet and found the kaolin preparation for diarrhoea and the vitamin syrup. After several doses, his diarrhoea seemed no better. The only other suitable medication I had was the antibiotic, *Penbritin,* which I was reluctant to administer unless his condition worsened.

We still didn't know what ailed him. Worriedly, we looked at the chart to see what port we might head for in an emergency. Morehead City, in North Carolina (USA), our destination, was closest – a mere 1,100 kilometres and at least seven days' sailing away!

Then Jamie came out in spots! Both Spock and The Ship Captains' Medical Guide were consulted several times before, with much relief, I came to the conclusion that he had German Measles (Rhubella). The spots began to fade after two days and soon Jamie's normally cheerful smile reappeared.

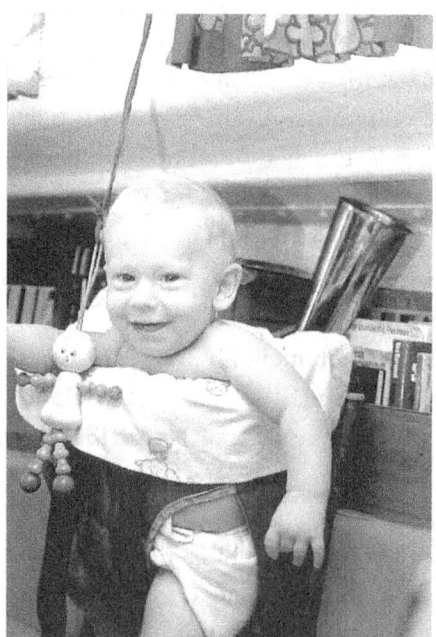

Jamie in his backpack in the cabin

Jamie sitting in cockpit
The car seat was a gift from Venus

Usually when we are sailing, we troll a fishing line behind the boat. Several big, gaily coloured Dorado took our hook in the Atlantic. They make delicious eating and are a welcome change from canned fish and meats. Although for us, bringing in the catch is a moment of excitement, not so for Jamie. Inevitably, I would be feeding him when the fish bit. The poor little boy would be removed from the breast, thrust into his cot (what would the psychologists say?) and the companionway door shut to keep the blood from splashing inside as the fish flailed on the cockpit floor.

Later on, of course, Jamie would enjoy a taste of fresh fish, too, It was a good source of protein and minerals for him, since I did not feed him any canned meat or vegetables or jars of baby food during his first year.

Once Jamie was mobile, our life became more complicated and he took up more and more space until, by the end of the voyage, we felt *Caprice* was bursting at the seams.

We replaced his cane cot with a small bunk slung in the forward cabin when he was 10 months old. Netting was attached right up to the deck-head, so that he couldn't get out, and the shelf alongside became his space for toys. As he grew taller, he used to pull himself up and peer out the open hatch. Later, he took great delight in throwing his toys out onto the deck.

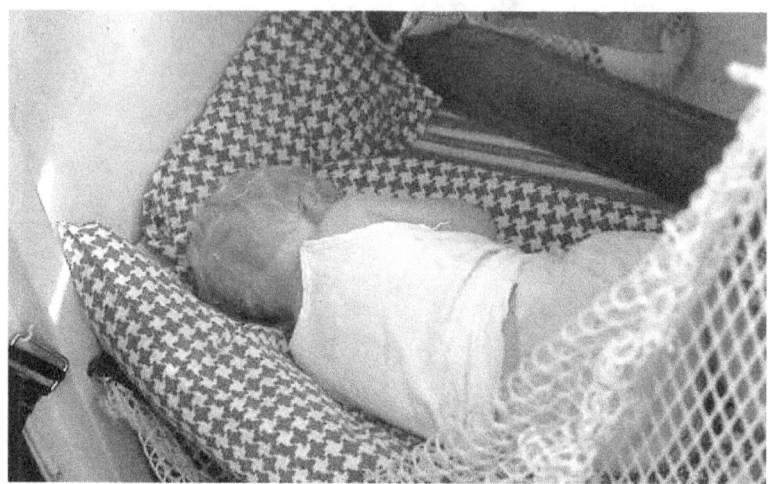

Jamie's new cot. The netting hooks to the deckhead

Most children love water play. Jamie was fascinated by the way the water welled in and out of the cockpit drain-holes. He spent hours pouring water from one container to another, so that the person on watch was forever filling the bucket for him. Then he started trying to fill it by himself – okay in port, but not so good when we were under way, because we were likely to lose the bucket overboard and maybe Jamie with it.

As soon as Jamie learned to walk and climb, we insisted he should never go into the cockpit or on deck without a harness or life-jacket. Fortunately, on none of the three occasions when he has fallen overboard were we at sea. The first time we were anchored in a channel at West Palm Beach in the US. Jamie was 13 months old, cumbersome in his life-jacket. He fell through the railing at the bow. Ian was ashore with the dinghy at the time, so it took considerable effort and much adrenalin for me to get us both aboard again.

For the next few months we took greater care and, of course, Jamie became more agile on deck. We reached Papéété in French Polynesia before he fell in again – twice in the course of 10 days. The last time he was wearing neither life-jacket nor harness. Ian and I were both on deck with him and we had him out of the water again so quickly, I think he didn't have time to realise what had happened.

It was in Papééte that I became pregnant for the second time – also according to plan. Because we wish to cruise extensively again we wanted the children sufficiently close in age to be companions. I had had no problems at all during my first pregnancy, so I assumed that I could cope with pregnancy at sea. It turned out that I couldn't! I was sick every time we sailed. By the time we reached Rarotonga in the Cook Islands after six days at sea, I was quite seriously dehydrated. I had been unable to take my usual tablets because they are unsuitable during pregnancy. I was 13 weeks pregnant and my weight had fallen lower than before conception.

Fortunately, the gynaecologist at Rarotonga was able to prescribe suitable medication so that during the remainder of our Pacific crossing I was able to keep the nausea under control. The passage from Rarotonga to New Zealand proved the worst of the whole voyage.

It was at this time that Jamie went through a stage of monkey-climbing. He delighted in standing on the bookshelf, grasping a handhold and peering through the window at the waves. Inevitably, as *Caprice* bounced off a wave, he lost his grip and was flung to the floor, landing on his temple. As a result, he suffered from concussion for two days.

Only a few days after the first incident, Jamie received another blow on the head. This time I had picked him up to put him to bed. *Caprice* lurched and I slipped. The back of Jamie's head and the bridge of my nose hit the edge of the bookshelf. There was the sound of bone cracking. When I examined Jamie's skull, he had a big black lump. Once again, Dr Spock was reassuring. The lump was from a broken capillary. I watched Jamie carefully for signs of shock, but to my surprise a few minutes later, I, not Jamie started to show damage. I had chipped the bone in my nose.

By way of compensation, we had a thoroughly enjoyable Tasman crossing to Australia to complete our 20,000 mile voyage with Jamie. My nausea eased and sailing conditions were very favourable. The passage took only eleven days.

Jamie on his second birthday in NZ

It was with regret on my part that we moved ashore a few days after our return to Sydney. The confine of a floating playpen, as we had nicknamed Caprice, was no place for the exuberance of a fast-developing two-year-old.

Jan, with Jamie and baby David

Footnote: Jan and Ian Mitchell's second son, David, was born last March (1928). Jamie is now two years and nine months old and the Mitchells are in the process of selling *Caprice* and buying a house. But they plan to buy a bigger yacht.

'Ian wants to go round Cape Horn and I want to sail the canals of Europe,' said Jan.

Part Three

Two Articles from Australian Sailing

February and August 1978

1 A Cruising Awakening

Jan Mitchell

Caprice sailing downwind at sea

Four years of sailing around the world taught this young Sydney couple much about their boat and about cruising. They voyaged across the Great Australian Bight to Western Australia; across the Indian Ocean to South Africa; then to the West Indies, east coast of the USA and finally home through Panama and across the Pacific.

'After all your experience, you'll find dodging the Sunday harbour sailors easy.'

'Oh yeah!' replied my circumnavigator husband, 'I'm more nervous of harbour sailing than any ocean crossing!'

I heartily endorse Ian's feelings. We might have sailed 28,000 sea miles across the three major oceans since leaving Sydney four years ago, but virtually none of that has involved harbour sailing. Like the majority of cruising yachties we met in our travels, before entering harbour, we lowered our sails, started the engine and motored into the anchorage. If we found more than half a dozen other yachts there, we felt that the place was crowded. Anyone who manoeuvred his boat under sail in confined waters was generally applauded. Moreover, once settled at anchor or tied up alongside a jetty, most cruising folk are very reluctant to make the effort to go day sailing except in their dinghies.

In our own case, with a boat as small as *Caprice* (LOA 7.5m), re-stowing of things used frequently in port took two hours or more. We slowly learned to be even more meticulous about stowing for a short sail than for a long passage – one leaves harbour, sets course and perhaps remains on the same tack for several days, whereas day sailing inevitably involves much tacking. On one occasion, my sewing box up-ended over the open engine compartment, resulting in a bilge pump diaphragm perforated by pins and needles. On another day excursion under all plain sail, we were stupidly caught by a southerly change which catapulted cutlery, ready-use galley stores, nuts, bolts and other assorted paraphernalia around the ears of two young boys who were guests aboard, while *Caprice*, out of control, plunged straight for the steel cliff of a moored ship.

A New Zealand yacht of our acquaintance nearly sank while day-sailing in Durban harbour. The crew had forgotten to close the port holes. Perhaps the explanation for this reluctance toward day sailing their own boats is that, like ourselves, many of the circumnavigators we met had done very little sailing before setting out. Ian had begun to dream of a small boat circumnavigation when, at 12 years of age, he read Bill Howell's *White Cliffs to Coral Reefs*. Thereafter, he read every cruising book upon which he laid eyes. By 15, he had taught himself the theory of celestial navigation and at 16, started to build a Bluebird in his parents back yard — all this without ever having been out sailing, even in a dinghy.

It was not until Ian reached 24, that an insurance payout for damages incurred in an accident gave him the capital that made the realisation of his dreams at all possible. He began looking at yachts with new zest. Then, in return for helping scrape and paint the underwater area of a 22 footer, we were taken for a day sail in Sydney Harbour – the first sailing experience for either of us.

A few months later on a wet Sunday afternoon a friend, who still remains among the dreamers, and Ian hired a Mirror dinghy for a few hours. Not long after, Ian and I purchased our first yacht, a 33ft steel sloop. The mistakes we made in our choice of boat and preparation for cruising make a story all of its own. During our 14 months of ownership, we sailed *Jenny II* three times in Pittwater and once outside. I was miserably seasick every time we ventured near the swell at Barrenjoey Head. It was an expensive lesson, but we were learning.

Caprice, a fibreglass Top Hat design, was our next boat, purchased only three months after the sale of the larger steel yacht. We have never regretted our choice. But then, our choice this time was the result of many hours spent considering every glass production boat on the market in eastern Australia. We had learned what to look for that would suit our needs: a rig that could be easily handled by one person, a relatively heavy displacement hull with a long keel, low maintenance yet strong construction, plenty of stowage space, an adequately sized water tank and full head room in the saloon for us both. All these, we found in the Top Hat.

Only eight months later, after day sailing *Caprice* three times and taking her to sea for an 18-day shake-down cruise, we had completed a few interior alterations, stowed the lockers and felt confident enough to set off on what became the first leg of our circumnavigation.

The rough weather and unexpectedly strong currents we had experienced on the shake-down cruise (when we managed to get within 15 miles of Lord Howe Island) made us extremely aware of planning for longer passages to be made at the times recommended in books such as *Ocean Passages for the World*, *Voyaging Under Sail* by Eric C. Hiscock, the various pilot books and routing charts issued by the British Hydrographic Office and the American pilot charts, as well as the published opinions of other ocean voyagers.

Our acquaintance with blue water sailors was virtually nil. The few people we knew who used the same marina were quite convinced we'd 'never make it', especially when they learned that we planned to reach the Indian Ocean via the Great Australian Bight rather than the more conventional Torres Strait route.

Our decision to go south was the result of several factors:

1. My term of employment was based on the calendar year.

2. The cost of living in Sydney was too high for us to remain there for several months waiting for the end of the cyclone season in

the Coral Sea.

3. With our lack of practical experience in sailing and navigation, we were reluctant to face the Coral Sea and Barrier Reef.

4. The available data suggested that in most years, easterly winds should prevail in the Great Australian Bight from mid-January until mid-March.

We decided to give the southern route a try and if we failed to make it through Bass Strait or to find the easterlies, it would still not be too late to go north,

We left Sydney in light conditions on February 5, 1974. The luck that stayed with us throughout the voyage began then. Apart from a southerly late the second day while we were still off the NSW coast, conditions could not have been more favourable. On the afternoon of our fifth day, we entered Bass Strait and from then until we overshot Fremantle and had to tack back, the wind was never forward of the beam.

Only two problems occurred during that two-stage hop round to Western Australia. Firstly, the water in the main tank continued to have a very bad flavour despite strong chemical treatment and cleaning of the tank before departure; and secondly, the engine continued to be unreliable. Ian had been unable to find the fault before we left Sydney and had given up in disgust.

During our two month stay at the CYC of WA, solutions to both problems were found. The engine fault turned out to be caused by a carbon-choked exhaust pipe, not an electrical fault as we had assumed.

To cure the strong plastic flavour of the water, Ian cut out the floor which forms the top of the tank, then used *Dynel* and epoxy to reline its glass interior. To his chagrin, however, the plastic flavour remained until I discovered that it was only in the water that had been sitting in the plastic pipe between the tank and the pump. The chief culprit was that piece of garden hose! After we replaced it with proper drinking-water, polythene piping, we had no more trouble.

While we were in Western Australia preparing for the Indian Ocean crossing, it occurred to us that the boat-shed receipt for *Caprice* was rather inadequate proof of our ownership, so we set about having her registered as a British Ship. How glad we were that we took this step. Every country we entered wanted to see our registration papers. The cost and trouble taken for the registration was minimal compared with the problems we could have encountered with no proper ownership documents when entering foreign ports.

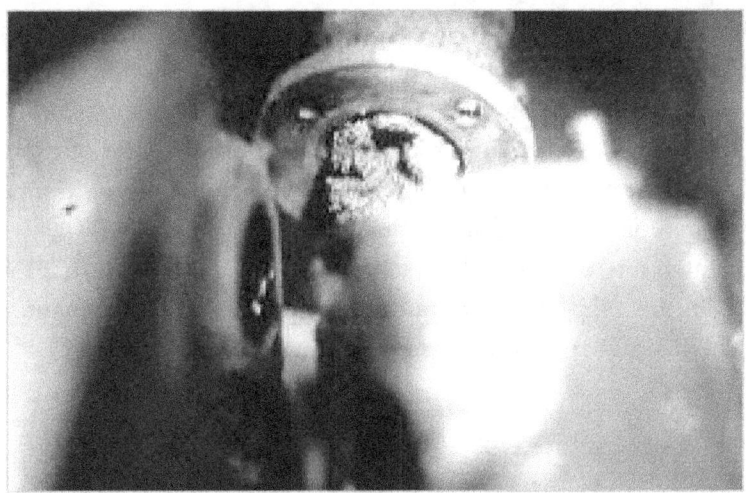

The Choked up Engine Exhaust Pipe

It was with tears and considerable misgivings that I saw the last view of the West Australian coast. For Ian, worry that he'd forgotten any last minute chores soon turned to elation. He is never more at peace with himself than when he is at sea. Ahead lay 3,600 sea miles of Indian Ocean, our goal, Rodriguez Island, a tiny dot in the seascape at Latitude S13°.

We found that tiny dot on the horizon over our bows 38 days later. Then I withdrew my last reservations about Ian's ability to use the plastic *Ebbco* sextant with enough accuracy to direct our course. Until the first sight of land, those small crosses on the chart had seemed quite unreal.

My faith in *Caprice* and ourselves grew steadily from that day on. Only two months later, I felt confident enough of my own ability to cope with cruising that I first suggested to Ian that we should have our first child in Durban, rather than wait until our return to Sydney. That way, I could work for a year, then be ready to leave South Africa when the baby was three months old. And so it was.

We arrived in Durban in August 1974, Jamie was born in November 1975 and we sailed from Cape Town in February 1976.

That 'teeny little baby who wouldn't take up much space' (my claim) soon converted *Caprice* into a floating nursery. For the next 18 months, we were daily faced with nappy washing. When Jamie started crawling and standing up at 10 months, and not much later, walking and climbing, *Caprice*'s dimensions seemed to shrink by three metres.

It is no wonder that our friends decided we had gone completely crazy when we carried out our plans for a second pregnancy, this time at sea, but with the baby due three and a half months after our return to Sydney. That experience, however, is one I have no desire to repeat. A combination of pregnancy nausea and seasickness largely incapacitated me for nearly three months. It seemed though that I was unlucky in this respect, for in Rarotonga, I met another pregnant first mate who had never experienced a moment of nausea at sea.

Yachts moored in Whangarei town basin, NZ

During the long weeks at sea, we have learned much about ourselves, our personal needs and desires and, of course, much about sailing. In port, too, we've passed happy hours discussing experiences with other cruising people. In particular, I have developed an interest in interior boat design for cruising (racing boats and their sailors are a different breed altogether with an entirely different set of needs), while Ian has become even more interested in hull design and rig. With these interests, we were always eager to visit other yachts to discuss the pros and cons of various features, then, back on board *Caprice*, to consider whether such features would suit our plans for another boat and another circumnavigation.

Yes! We definitely plan to 'take off' again, but next time it will be in a boat that will be our home, not a sea-going caravan; the crew will include our two by then school-age children and the routes we choose to follow will be a little further off the conventional track.

2 Lost
Ian Mitchell

The morning was bright and brisk as I guided *Caprice*, our 25 foot Top Hat sloop, north towards the entrance to Broken Bay and the open sea. Jan had just finished stowing away the last items and was now preparing breakfast before we hit the heavy swell outside. I was feeling, almost exclusively, relieved that all the frantic last-minute tasks had been completed and that at last the objective of the immediate future – to sail to Lord Howe Island and then return to Broken Bay – was stark and simple. Jan punctuated my mood of quiet exaltation by handing me breakfast; an omelette to which kippered herrings had been added. It didn't strike me as being the ideal breakfast but I said nothing and wolfed it down, reflecting that Jan must have considerable faith in her anti-seasick tablets. She had been seasick every time we had ventured outside the sheltered waters of Broken Bay for a couple of hours, the longest we had ever been "at sea". I had never been seasick.

After clearing Barrenjoey, we turned NE, intending to make sure that we weren't set south by the coastal current. The wind was fine on the quarter and steering required too much concentration in the big swell to avoid gybing, so we lowered the reefed main and bubbled along on the working jib alone. The coast moved slowly by and we watched it with the relief – almost disbelief – of actually having made it to sea, mixed with the beginnings of apprehension.

We lasted quite a while. It was an hour before Jan reached for the significantly-coloured yellow bucket and I lasted three whole hours more. Somehow, the untested QME self-steering was rigged and, dully, we appreciated its ease of adjustment and efficiency. Settling miserably in the cockpit, we passed the little yellow bucket to and fro at very frequent intervals. The smell of the kippered herring remnants in the frying pan and on the plates was definitely not helping our stomachs. So in the mid-afternoon, I forced myself down below to clean it all, by this time feeling that if the reek were not removed, we were both going to die of ruptured innards. It was only my Scot's ancestry that prevented me from hurling anything that had been in contact with kippered herrings into the sea.

By dusk, the wind had become lighter and the QME would no longer work with the small sail area; too sick to think of putting up more sail, we pulled it all down, not improving the motion, and I went below to be more comfortably sick in the warmth of my bunk. After an hour's cajoling, I managed to persuade Jan to lie down also.

Despite our resolve to stand watches, the novelty of seasickness had exhausted us too much and I was awakened by Jan yelling at me to get up as there were houselights close and we were about to go ashore. Before I'd untangled myself from the blankets, she yelled down, with no less urgency, that the lights were of a ship very close.

We both stood in the cockpit while an Aldis flashed in our faces at a bemusing rate (not that we could have read it even if it were much slower). Jan waved her arms about and yelled, trying to convey the message that we were quite alright and would he please clear off, while I dived below and tried to reach the ship on 2182 kHz. The freighter circled and came very close, sufficiently so that I could be heard as I bellowed up those steel cliffs. At last he was satisfied and moved on, leaving us giggling weakly with relief. (The merchant ships were very interested in us on this and other occasions, presumably because a small yacht on passage from New Zealand to Sydney had been reported missing and a full alert was out.)

At dawn we set course east to clear the coast and shipping lanes. Jan concocted a hot drink of chocolate, glucose and condensed milk, which remained for a reasonable time in our thankful stomachs.

I tried my first-ever sextant sight, worked it and found the position line passed within 12 nautical miles of the position given by bearings on the coast. The seasickness was leaving us by the afternoon, although the wind had become stronger and the swell higher. The self-steering was continuing to work well with the wind on the quarter and only the working jib up.

An hour or two after dusk, while both of us were sitting below, *Caprice* suddenly broached and violently rolled to some-where near the horizontal, projecting me across the cabin and collecting Jan's mouth with the top of my head. Both horrified, we slowly separated but there were no broken tooth, although her lip was badly split.

Renewed seasickness.

Soon after, we replaced the working jib with the storm jib, with which the QME would still handle her, leaving us down below and trying to get some sleep.

The navigation lights failed due to poor installation; an insignificant incident which assumed vast proportions in our wearied, but ever-active imaginations. The weather gradually deteriorated and several rain showers passed over. By mid-morning, the sea was short and steep, to the extent that the QME could no longer hold *Caprice* as she surged on the crests. Occasional wave tops lopped into the cockpit and water found its way below.

We took turns at steering, teaching ourselves how to catch her to prevent broaching while using the minimum of effort and to distinguish between those waves which could be disregarded and those which had to be met exactly stern on. In daylight this was quite pleasant and there was the interest in learning a new skill. But at dusk, fear and depression came rushing back.

After three hours of darkness, we convinced ourselves that conditions had eased. We put the QME back to work and crept below, where there was the artificial sun of the cabin light, to huddle in our hunks. At 2am there was a sharp crack followed by a violent broach and roll and I rushed out to find the control ropes to the tiller had snapped and that the whipping ends had carried away the radio aerial. I steered in front of the sea, eyes straining in the overcast and moonless night, to see the direction of the crests and occasionally wrenching *Caprice* around to put her stern into a peaking cross sea.

Conditions became rapidly worse in the next hour. My imagination was full of *Caprice* pitch-poling. Even in our inexperience, we could see that she was going too fast down the steep faces, the log often registering $8 \frac{1}{2}$ knots as she surged behind her constantly backing 35 square feet of storm jib.

The tiller was hard work and I could not grasp the energy to think or act constructively. Instead, I sat intensely hoping that conditions would ease. Finally we were broached badly, this time rolling past the horizontal, and we skidded broadside down the wave. Once again I careered into Jan who energetically pushed me back into my seat almost before *Caprice* lurched upright. Jan had saved me from going clean over the guardrail.

The cockpit was half full of water and we grabbed buckets and bailed madly, the inadequate cockpit drains having been further reduced by the sheet tails washing down them. After most of the water was tossed out, Jan went below, mopped up the few gallons that had made it over the storm board, wedged the books, food and kitchen utensils bank into their racks, shelves and cupboards and returned to the cockpit.

The jib had to come down, but there was no chance of my going up on the foredeck because Jan had not the strength to hold the tiller. The storm jib was snapping from side to side and this action had worked half the piston hanks free of the forestay. For a short while I hoped the sail might disintegrate to save us the trouble, but there was little chance of that.

Finally Jan went forward. It was a bad few minutes. In the darkness I could not see her even if I could spare the time to look forward, and the noise of wind and sea was such that she could not have heard my warning if I spotted a real rogue wave. I felt *Caprice's* speed ease slightly and the flogging of the sail stopped. Then, at last, Jan dropped into the cockpit beside me.

We ran on under bare poles but the removal of the storm jib had not slowed *Caprice* much and she was still going much too fast, demanding both feet on the tiller between waves to stop her broaching.

It was only a matter of time before we would be caught again. The idea of towing warps presented itself but it would take many minutes (and much effort!) to run them out and I wasn't at all sure that the little stern cleats would take the stress. So we picked a smooth patch, turned *Caprice* broadside and hunched tensely as the next big sea came. But she rose easily and only the very top of the wave slapped the sides. We slowly relaxed. Occasionally a peaking cross sea gave her a frightening thump which wrenched her around 45° or smashed down on the foredeck. With the tiller lashed to leeward, she behaved just like the "how to sail" books had described lying ahull except, perhaps, for the unpleasantness of cross seas. We went below, straining our ears for the sound of the wave that would pick up *Caprice*, hurl her into the trough and smash on top of her.

Jan lay uncomfortably on her bunk with her life-jacket over the top of her safety harness webbing, over her water-proofs, over her layer of woollens. The sight irritated me to the point of making the extremely unkind remark to the effect that a life-jacket would only prolong the agony if *Caprice* went down.

The cabin light began to dim because of lack of battery power and our spirits dropped with it. Jan fervently stated once more that if we survived she would never again go out of Broken Bay in a yacht. I retained enough sense not to argue with her, or perhaps I was too exhausted. I managed to stir myself into disengaging the centrifugal clutch and starting the engine by hand – an occupation that took a long time and which distracted both of us from our principal preoccupation.

Our confidence grew as, at first light, we watched the high steep waves bearing down on us, felt momentarily as if we were in an elevator as *Caprice* accelerated up the slope, almost floating clear over the crest, leaving no more than a bucketful of white water to slop into the cabin sides. The sea had become more regular in the last hour of darkness but it was still high and very steep, seemingly out of proportion to the wind.

Jan managed to hold a pot on the stove long enough to heat a can of stew. With the warmth of food inside us, we brightened in outlook and the half-despairing lassitude slipped away. I took an astonishingly consistent set of sun sights. Jan mended a tear in the storm jib where a piston hank had punched a hole, and we rearranged the scattered stores.

The weather continued to moderate and in the early afternoon, we very cautiously hoisted the working jib. In two hours, the sea had dropped to a third of its previous size, despite scarcely any drop in the wind. We slowly increased sail until next day we were becalmed in a near flat sea. When I went over the side to unwind a rope from around the propeller shaft, the water was so clear and blue that I momentarily hesitated to let go the rail, feeling I would fall as in air.

The next couple of days were spent very pleasantly in mild conditions under a sunny sky and we happily told each other that this was what cruising was all about. I found a 30 minute error in the plastic sextant, probably induced when the sextant box was flung onto the cabin floor a couple of days previously.

On the mid-morning of the seventh day out, I told Jan we should see Lord Howe just before dusk. Jan spotted the island two hours later and, in her (rather insulting) joyful amazement, overlooked the fact that the navigator was fifteen nautical miles out.

The day was just short of being a sailing ideal. The breeze was somewhat light, but the two nearly equal peaks grew slowly out of the horizon while we did odd jobs and read up about the island.

The photo Australian Sailing published. We didn't get so close to Lord Howe I.

Just before dusk, we were surprised by an anti-submarine frigate accompanied by a Daring Class destroyer of the Australian navy, crossing our stern at a couple of nautical miles distance. Later, in the waning light, the black shape of an Oberon Class submarine followed them.

Fearful of coming too close to the unlighted island, we pulled down sail soon after sunset and gained a good night's sleep. At dawn, we were on deck straining our eyes, but the sun was well up before we spotted the island. To our sinking disappointment, we realised that we had been set well south by a current during the night and were now about forty miles SW of the island.

The wind swung straight into our faces and began to strengthen. Rather bad tempered, we tried to slam *Caprice* to windward, but to no avail. We tried the engine as well, but the increase in speed was negligible. There was no chance of making headway directly towards the island under engine alone in the increasing sea.

By late afternoon, bearings on Lord Howe and the elemental shape of Ball's Pyramid told us we'd covered about 18 nautical miles during daylight hours. Dusk came and with it, lashing rain and bright electrical activity. Jan kept flinching at the thunder and flashes and I made a mental note to earth the mast if and when we returned to land.

A short council of war decided that we would give up any attempts to reach Lord Howe and head back to the Australian coast. This was the end of our eighth day at sea and time was running out. We both had only two weeks leave from our jobs. In spite of a good night's rest, the energy simply ran out of us once the decision was taken and morale sank.

We hove *Caprice* to* – the first time we had tried this – and as the wind came round to the north from the NE, she slowly fore-reached westward over a moderate sea. Lord Howe was still visible in the dawn of the next day. By afternoon, we were becalmed again. The next four days were spent changing sails frequently and trying to force *Caprice* into head winds and seas that were far too much for her. One day, we spent ten hours on the tiller to gain ten miles on the log.

*To *heave to* involves lashing the tiller to keep the sails backed. Lying ahull is similar, but with no sail up.

For twenty-four hours, our hand held wind metre registered a steady forty knots when, on the top of a larger sea, we held it above the cabin top. The seas were large but regular and no longer frightened us. They became merely an impediment to progress. Sextant sights indicated we were being taken north no matter what we did to press westwards.

The tank water had become almost undrinkable due to algae growth. Jan had difficulty keeping this water down, even after it had been boiled. We had little other water, so that minor dehydration, made worse by the reflexive licking of salt encrusted lips, was taking almost unnoticed effect.

The task of setting the mainsail was becoming exhausting. Having no main halyard winch, nor any purchase, I once took more than an hour to haul the luff taut on the double reefed main, while being helped as much as possible by Jan, who sat at the tiller luffing *Caprice* to and fro through the wind.

On the fifth day after turning back, when the wind turned easterly and moderated, we at last moved westward. A couple of hours before dawn we sighted the loom of a light house. The light came very quickly out of the sea and we realised we were coming up to the coast more rapidly than the five knots registered on the log. We could not identify the light. (This was not surprising as our lights information had been published fifteen years before.)

We passed through the shipping lanes in the early dawn, dodging a freighter that had not a soul in sight, bridge or deck. We closed with the coast to stare at it in puzzlement. We managed to convince ourselves that the coast before us was, magically, just north of Port Stephens. (By this stage, we were feeling rather helpless in our negotiation of the strong currents with which we were contending and resorted to optimism.)

We turned south and when the sun was high enough, a position line revealed that we were only a few miles south of Coolangatta. We had been pushed 180nm off our intended course since leaving the vicinity of Lord Howe.

I headed a page in the log "Coastal Navigation from Coolangatta." By midday we passed Cape Byron, the most easterly point of Australia. We knew the cape quite well from a visit by land and were now close enough to see the goats perched on the steep green slopes above the vertical drop on the southern side of the lighthouse. This sighting was a good confirmation of the celestial position line.

An hour after passing Cape Byron, we were under bare poles and managing somehow to head SE away from the coast as a black nor'easter hit. At times during the afternoon, we made four and a half knots with no sail up. It was a moderately miserable, wet night; we were right in the shipping lanes, so both of us stayed in the cockpit, one on the tiller staring at the poorly lit compass, while the other looked out for ships. We saw several and one altered course towards us and signalled with an Aldis, to which Jan flashed back with a torch OK, OK, OK...

While it was still dark, the wind began to moderate and we set the jib and headed back towards the coast. But soon after dawn, the wind backed right round to the SW and began quickly to strengthen. We soon gave up trying to press *Caprice* to windward and, after setting the trysail to steady the rolling, we laid her on the starboard tack and went down below to sleep restlessly and worry about our food and water.

By dawn of the next day the wind and sea had moderated and we set sail due west. A near noon sight put us at exactly S33°, 240 nautical miles south of our previous day's noon position! I felt like solemnly thumping my head against something solid. The sight was so close to noon that no real error was induced by working it as a noon-sight and this I did with the same result. I carefully checked the sextant and shot the sun again. The same result! Great elation mixed with a niggling worry that I was going round the twist. Not daring to estimate our longitude, we continued west, making slightly facetious yet anxious comments about how if this current continued we might find ourselves in Antarctica.

The afternoon sight gave us a position about 70 nautical miles off the coast and we altered course NW to counter the current and avoid being set south of Sydney. This bearing happened to pass through Port Stephens. While actually taking the sight, the sea changed from a short, sharp, white, little chop to a gentle low swell. It was a startling transition. Happily we noted the beginning of city haze on the horizon as the sun sank and we pressed *Caprice* on as hard as we could, occasionally using the engine as the wind slackened.

Three hours before dawn we were rewarded with a light dead ahead. Again we could not identify the light and after sunrise, we approached it closely enough to see the structure, but that did not help the identification either, We argued the pros and cons for being, north or south of Sydney and Jan had just convinced me that we had been taken far south by the current and so should turn north, when we spotted a fishing boat to which, after same rather clumsy effort, we managed to close.)

'Where the hell are we?'

'Port Stephens. There's the light over there!' Didn't all the world know Port Stephens light?

Jan and I stared at each other wonderingly. For the first time since we'd put to sea, the current had not interfered. We had laid a course, kept on the bearing and arrived where we should have. We realised that the sharp transition we had experienced the previous afternoon when taking the sight was, in fact, the boundary of the southerly set. We turned south down the coast wondering rather superstitiously what was going to be the next bolt fired at us to offset our extreme good luck.

Ian winching up the mainsail

The wind increased slowly from the west, but we were hugging the coast too closely for much wave build up and with about 20 nautical miles still to go to Broken Bay, were moving along happily, although reduced to storm jib and trysail. The radio mentioned a minor change from the south and we watched cautiously as one dark roll of cloud passed over, than another. We started to relax and think about putting up more sail, then suddenly grabbed for handholds as *Caprice* heeled about 70° in the strongest gust we had so far experienced.

I crawled up forward, doused the jib, left *Caprice* to fend for herself laid to with the trysail up, and went below. Jan heated our second last can of soup. By the time we had eaten, the narrow cold front had passed and we set sail again.

Midnight found us slowly tacking up towards the light at the entrance to Broken Bay. It was a moonless but clear night and we stood in towards the light, but than my nerve failed me and we turned and went seaward again and, tacking to and fro, waited for the dawn.

The morning was a truly beautiful, golden quiet. There was just enough breeze to send us in towards the two dimensional facade of Broken Bay, which opened and gained depth as we came nearer and the sun rose, revealing the promontories and island we knew so well.

Part Four

A History of Top Hat Yachts

Jan Mitchell

TOP HAT 25

25.00' / 7.62m 1963

John Illingworth and Angus Primrose

In the 1950's, the English Yacht design firm, Illingworth and Primrose, designed the Top Hat. In 1963 Rob Legge and partner (RL Yachts) were approached to build an initial six boats for the newly formed JOG racing fleet in Port Phillip Bay. The six original boats were built from cold moulded timber: five 3 mm laminations laid up with resorcinol glue on Mahogany stem and main frame, with laminated mahogany floors. The vessel boasted a long keel and a keel hung rudder.

Right from the start John Illingworth proved to be the most cooperative designer Legg had worked with. 'Nothing was too much trouble, and he had a vast practical experience,' said Legg. (Source: Top Hat website)

From a 1960's newspaper clipping:
Top Hat Dips its Lid

Meet Top Hat, the new 25 ft. Illingworth and Primrose design moulded plywood cruiser-racer, adopted by the Junior Offshore Group of Victoria, which will dip its lid to Australian yachtsmen for the first time on Port Phillip Bay this season.

The group formed a co-operative of potential owners to order a mould and bulk buy components and fittings. *Mouldcraft* of Frankston are completing the last two hulls of the six the group ordered in its original scheme and have also received orders for another seven or eight, including one from NSW. The first two to hit the water, owned by group secretary Bob Moon and David Cockburn, should be launched at Sandringham early in November. Nine or ten could be racing on the Bay by the end of the season.

The Top Hat is moulded in five-ply construction of 9/16ths (15 mm) thickness, has accommodation for four, with 5 ft. 9 in. (175 cm) headroom in the saloon, an adequate galley and self-draining cockpit.

Details:
- Length over-all, 25.1 ft.
- Length waterline, 21 ft.
- Beam (max.), 8 ft.
- Draft, 4.25 ft.
- Displacement, 2.54 tons.
- Lead keel, 1.25 tons.
- Sail area, 286 sq. ft.

(Source: Top Hat website.)

~

Geoff Baker:

During the 1960's, Geoff Baker, a traditional timber shipwright, was working at the Royal Brighton Yacht Club in Melbourne. He was familiar with the timber Top Hats. Towards the end of the 1960's, he came to Sydney to work for **Bill Jeffries**, who owned *Fibreglass Yachts* in Mona Vale. They consulted with John Illingworth about building a fibreglass version of the Top Hat.

Jeffries brought a wooden Top Hat to Sydney. Baker took a fibreglass mould from the upturned hull. This mould was turned right side up and another mould was taken from its interior. The second copy became the mould for the hull of the new boats, which became known as the Mark I Top Hat yacht.

In Australia during the 1960's, the use of glass-fibre reinforced plastic for boats was new and experimental. Baker hand-laid the hull over the outside of the mould and reinforced it with glassed in wooden stringers. Therefore the boats he built are considered to be stronger than the later models, where a spray gun was used to apply chopped-strand glass fibre. Baker used timber for the interior fit-out.

The original timber Top Hats had a sliding hatch above the companionway. The cabin profile had a step-down to the mast. The sheet winches were mounted on steel struts. Some had a double spreader rig. For standard accommodation, there were four berths, a centrally located galley and a large chart table, as Illingworth placed great importance on the role of the navigator.

The new fibreglass version (Mark I) followed most of the original timber version, but had a "key-hole" entry (semi-elliptical shaped cabin top above companionway). The main-sheet traveller was located above the companionway, usually a raised stainless steel tube following the contour of the cabin top. Another version had no traveller, just a ring bolt amidships through the cabin top. The sheet winches were located on fibreglass mounts on the cockpit coaming. A narrow sheet of stainless steel covered the deck/hull join and wooden rubbing strakes were fixed to the outer hull. The enclosed head, twin-berths forward, central galley and settee berths port and starboard were retained. Against the bulkhead for the head, a table was fitted. It could be secured up when the bunk was in use or fixed down to be used as a chart table. The settee berths passed a short distance aft under the cockpit seats. Two large, opening cockpit lockers took up the remaining space under the cockpit seats.

There were two options for engine power. A large removable section of the stern coaming allowed for a reinforced outboard mount to be incorporated. Aft of the saloon, provision was made for a small engine under the cockpit floor, with access via a removable step at the companionway. The RCA Dolphin 12hp petrol engine was one such engine fitted and the small Stuart Turner petrol engine was offered as an alternative. Some owners installed a small Yanmar diesel when it became available. The propeller aperture was cut out of the keel hung rudder.

Altogether, from 1968 to 1974, when Baker retired, he built approximately 56 Top Hat yachts. These are the prized Mark I Baker-Built yachts.

Jeffries took the Top Hat moulds to Warriewood and for a couple of years, tried to reduce the costs of construction. Only a few more boats were built using Baker's system before the business relocated to Wyong on the Central Coast of NSW, and the firm's name changed to *Formit Fibreglass*. There they built a new version of the boat and employed Mike Garrett and subsequently, Merv Howlett as salesmen.

The Mark II Top Hat was first released in 1976 with a wider and fatter cabin top. The hull shape was retained, but the interior layout was modernised with a fibreglass shell, reducing much of the time consuming timber fitting out. The deck was also streamlined and the new method of spray gun layup was introduced. The Mast step-down was curved, the forward hatch was relocated, and an anchor-well installed. Also, the window shape was altered to give a more streamlined impression.

The Mark III version appeared around 1981 and usually had a single sleek tinted acrylic glass window on either side of the cabin. However the traditional windows of three per side could be specified. Two interior designs were available. The A is the racing version with the head between the forward bunks and a hanging locker in the main saloon for wet weather gear etc. The B is a fully enclosed head version, with toilet and hand basin, aimed at the small family cruising market. A single deep cockpit locker was provided on the port side which allowed for a good sized quarter berth on the starboard side.

~

The following information was kindly supplied to the Top Hat website by Merv Howlett, former salesman for Formit Fibreglass: *Merv has given his permission for it to be repeated here.*

'The basic hull of the Mark III remained the same with the near full length keel and a keel hung rudder. Ballast of 1234 kg (2721 lb) of lead in the keel and a displacement of 2580 kg (5688 lb), makes a safe ballast ratio of 48%. The hulls were gun sprayed in two halves, joined down the middle and then lead poured into the keel from the inside.

There were shallow draft versions built in Mk 2 & 3. A 10" high plug was inserted into the mould and the then extra ballast added to give the same performance. Bill Jeffries owned *Fibreglass Yachts* Later renamed *Formit Fibreglass*. (He changed the name to *Formit* when the company moved to Wyong under a government grant scheme to move factories out of Sydney). Mike Garratt was the salesman before Merv Howlett. 500 + Top Hats originated from *Fibreglass Yachts* and *Formit*. Some were built in Victoria, the exact number is unknown.

A lot of Top Hats were completed by their owners. Caution should be exercised with these vessels as a number left the factory as a separate hull and deck. Always check the deck connection to the hull in these vessels.

Some Mark 3's had three windows and not one long one. All timbers encased in fibreglass were of pine and ordinary plywood. Mast steps (about $600) are still available from *Marine Installations*, The cabin floor was lowered in the Mark 2 & 3 to maintain the head room; some home completed versions may vary.

The most important structural part of a Top Hat is the bulkhead under the mast.

The ballast developed over three phases (changes caused by cost).

Phase 1. A 1 piece cast lead moulding fibre-glassed in.

Phase 2. A 2 piece cast lead moulding fibre-glassed in.

Phase 3. 20lb lead ingots set in cement slurry and glassed in.

Eventually, the company ceased to produce Top Hat yachts, including the Top Hat 27, which was of a different design. The Top Hat moulds were sold and sent to Queensland and *Formit* moved into producing other fibreglass products (including portable toilets) and today, they no longer build boats."

~

Bill Jeffries sold *Formit Fibreglass* in 2005. *Central Coast Marine Installations* is still in business.

Jay Jay, formerly moored on Lake Macquarie NSW, is possibly the first boat to have come out of the moulds. She was numbered '3'. A former owner, Bob Cowdrey, sanded the hull back for re-coating, finding the imprint of the timber planking on his hull. *Jay Jay* was sold in mid-2012 and taken to Botany Bay.

Caprice was built in 1969. She was four years old when we purchased her in June, 1973. She lacked a traveller and we fitted a straight stainless steel one above her companionway. She has fibreglass mounts for her sheet winches, an enclosed head opposite the galley and a step-down to the mast fitting. Her rig has a single spreader. There were wooden rubbing strakes along the sides of the hull, but as these contained some rot, Ian and I removed them. We made a plywood vee to fit between the twin forward bunks, creating a large forward storage platform. The other important alteration we made before departing Sydney was to make a very solid chart table.

Ian was determined to have somewhere he could lay out flat a whole chart. He built a wide table right above the starboard settee, with drawers beneath it: one full width for the charts and two half width for navigation equipment and stationary. There was just enough room left underneath the drawers for an adult to roll into the bunk.

In the United States, we built a pipe berth above the port side of the forward cabin for baby Jamie. Heavy netting hooked up to the deck head kept him secure and he used the bookcase alongside his bunk for his toys. (See photo p.134.)

In November 1995, when our son Jamie had not long turned 20, he bought *Possibilities*, a Mark I Top Hat built in 1972. This vessel had no inboard engine; otherwise, it was very similar to *Caprice*, with an enclosed toilet compartment. Jamie lived aboard at Balls Head Bay and Berry's Bay for three years while he completed his degree in Environmental Science and Geography at Macquarie University. In late January 1999, after a furious two months of preparations, he set off to circumnavigate the world, returning ten years later in December 2008.

Our younger son, David, bought *Ratu V,* a Mark II Top Hat in the summer of 1998/9. With Jamie as crew, he sailed her to Lake Macquarie and lived aboard for a year during his engineering studies at Newcastle University. To us, her construction appeared less robust than that of *Caprice* or *Possibilities*. David sold *Ratu V* again the following summer.

~

Advertising for the Top Hat from Fibreglass Yachts:

TOP HAT ~ An outstanding yacht in every way.
FIBREGLASS YACHTS (SALES) PTY. LTD. 9 Perak Street, MONA VALE, N.S.W., 2103 Phone: 997 -6289

A thoroughbred offshore Cruising/Racing Yacht, the Top Hat utilizes the highest standards of construction in Fibreglass, to the specifications of the designers Illingworth & Primrose.

The Top Hat's proven performance, ease of handling and amazing interior accommodation make her an ideal yacht for family cruising.

Durability Investment Protection:

Depreciation is practically eliminated in a well-designed boat of fibreglass construction. Completely impervious to the ravages of rot, rust, corrosion, electrolysis, water absorption and marine borers.

Maintenance Savings:

This is a vital factor in a yacht of this size. The savings grow with the length of ownership, as permanent, moulded-in colours and seam-free hull minimize annual painting, scraping, caulking and other annual yard bills. For the racing sailor, the Top Hat has an excellent record and with her short overhangs, well-designed hull form and "stiffness" has proved to be an outstanding performer in both round the buoys and offshore racing.

Standard Specifications:

Hull:

Round Bilge, constructed completely of fibreglass, with 2,500 Ib. of lead ballast moulded within the keel section. This gives the advantage of tremendous strength and avoids any possibility of leaks occurring through keel bolts.

Cabin, Deck & Cockpit:

Moulded in fibreglass, chemically bonded and riveted to the hull, thus making a single integral unit of great strength. No leaks can occur through cabin top or deck and the boat is always dry.

Colours:

Selected colours are "moulded in" to ensure enduring appearance.

Accommodation:

Interior appointments are both pleasing and functional. Full standing headroom, 2 settee berths in the main cabin, 2 full-length berths in the forward cabin, a well-equipped galley with stove, stainless steel sink and fresh water pump, storage cupboards and a cutlery drawer

Toilet:

The marine toilet is contained within a separate cabin. Sea cocks are fitted to all external openings, ensuring complete safety from leaks in the event of a pipe breaking.

Fresh Water Tank:

Located in the keel section, with a capacity of 35 gallons, lined with epoxy resin, and inspection hatch provided.

Ventilation:

The forward cabin hatch cover is hinged and has a waterproof vent to provide fresh air movement through the cabin when closed.

The cabin door is also ventilated, ensuring movement of air through the boat when moored.

Cockpit:

Self-draining and can comfortably seat six. Each seat incorporates a large locker sealed from the hull interior. Main hatchway is fitted with lockable fibreglass door.

Anti-Skid:

All deck areas and the cockpit sole have anti-skid pattern moulded in. Chain-Plates

Eight stainless steel chain plates are bolted through the deck in areas specially reinforced to distribute the loads.

Mast Head Rig:

This gives the yacht a wide choice of headsails for optimum performance and balance under a wide variety of wind and sea conditions. The Alloy Mast is stepped on deck, giving unhindered access to the forward cabin.

Standard Rigging:

1 x 19 Stainless Steel with swaged terminals. Running Rigging:

7 x 19 Stainless Steel with synthetic rope tails. Synthetic Jib and Main Sheets.

Deck Fitting:

Two Jib Sheet winches and cleats. Jib sheet slides on stainless steel tracks. Stem head fitting with mooring line roller. Bow fairleads. Anchor line pipe through deck. Bow mooring cleat. Main sheet eye.

Rudder:

Timber completely covered with fibreglass, stainless steel stock with swivelling tiller

Optional Extras Available: Choice of inboard engines. Forward windows in main cabin. Provision for outboard motor.

Vents.

Forward stowage shelves Bilge pump.
Table. Topping lift.
Main cabin lockers. Rub rail.
Main cabin shelves.

Pulpits, stanchions & life lines. Bunk lee boards.
Priming and antifouling. Boot top.
Bunk cushions.

Addendum

Jan and Ian Mitchell in 2012

Jan and Ian Mitchell did not realise their dream of cruising the world with their children. A house, mortgage and two jobs became a reality check for them. They did buy a Phantom 32 they called *Realitas*, which became their holiday home and in that yacht, they sailed as a family to Tasmania, Lord Howe (several times) and New Zealand, as well as up and down the NSW coast.

The Mitchell boys have grown up, married and have their own yachts. Jamie bought a Top Hat, *Possibiilities,* and spent ten years sailing the world. Now he and wife Lisa sail *The Wild Goose* with baby Tane and crew. David prefers multihulls, especially catamarans, and has owned several boats. He currently owns *Halcyon Daze,* and lives in Newcastle with his wife and son.

Meanwhile, Jan and Ian have their sixth yacht, a Brolga 33 called *Osprey A*, moored 200m from their retirement home on the shores of Lake Macquarie, and have continued to ocean sail. To Ian's disappointment, Jan, at 65, has decided after their most recent cruise, that her body is no longer up to sailing at sea.

Jan's passion in her retirement is more writing. In 2011, she published a biography of a remarkable Australian, *tinker, tailor, soldier, sailor…the life of Colin Kerby OAM.*

See Jan's website, **writingsfromjanmitchell.com** for more about her writing projects.

She has been President of the Lake Macquarie branch of the Fellowship of Australian Writers and enjoys helping edit other writers' work.

www.ingramcontent.com/pod-product-compliance
Lightning Source LLC
Chambersburg PA
CBHW071920290426
44110CB00013B/1421